BLACK MEXICO

[A beggar in the central market village of Cuajinicuilapa, Mexico]

The Greatest Story Never Told

To manipulate history is to manipulate consciousness; to manipulate consciousness is to manipulate possibilities; and to manipulate possibilities is to manipulate power.....

*From the introduction to the **Falsification of Afrikan Consciousness**, by Amos Wilson.*

Black Mexico: The Greatest Story Never Told
Second Edition
© 2016 W.O.M.B. PUBLICATIONS, LLC

ISBN-13: 978-099605-4966
ISBN-10: 099605 4960

"Giving Birth to the Best Books on Earth!"

W.O.M.B. PUBLICATIONS, Jersey City, NJ
Editor-in-Chief: Raymond S. Muhammad

All rights reserved. No part of this book may be reproduced or transmitted in any form or by any means, electronic or mechanical, without permission in writing from the publisher.

Inquiries to Co-publisher:

Ancient Geographic Expressions Systems, Inc.

1 West Prospect Avenue #144
Mount Vernon, NY 10550 U.S.A.
e-mail: ancientmexico@gmail.com

Lamont Ramor Curry, 1949-
Black Mexico: The Greatest Story Never Told
by Lamont (Ra-Muur Khu-Re) Muhammad
Part II of the A.G.E.S. Demystification series.

This expanded edition includes appendices that are newspaper and magazine articles the author penned on related subjects since the pamphlet edition (2000). They were contributed to *The Final Call, Black Diaspora Magazine, New York Amsterdam News, New York Beacon, New York Carib News*, and online @ *The Black World Today* (www.tbwt.org). The pieces have been edited to better explain and to limit repetition where possible. The datelines reflect when the articles were originally submitted to said publications. The final appendix is offered as charity and a frame of reference to support the theme of this project.

Includes bibliographical notes and illustrations.

History:

First Edition- Library of Congress Cataloging-in-Publication Data
ISBN 0-9771208-0-5
SAN 256.8039

Copyright © 2000, 2005, 2015, Lamont R. Curry

In the Name of the Lord of All of the Worlds!

This project is dedicated to the memory of
my mother, Jacqueline Ingrams;
and my father, Alonzo Curry.

Foreword

Imhotep (Peace and Harmony)!

First of all it's an honor to introduce this insightful piece of work that furthered my understanding of the African presence in Mexico before Christopher Columbus. We know that the African presence goes back and that the first Mayans were Africans...

I love the research that went into the writing of *Black Mexico*... It was very good because now we do not have to take anybody else's word for the facts. We can go back and look at the major cities that are documented in this text. We can look at the museums. We can look at those particular authors that were brought forth in the book. This is what young people need.

I guess Brother Lamont, being a journalist, is a boost because documented evidence is what our young people need. Our history has been denied or blocked out of our history books but this book brings a lot of light to the surface. I was impressed by some of the people who were interviewed to get this information. This is good because we need to know our history from several different angles.

At the risk of repeating myself, I really respect the book because it documents the African presents in Mexico before Columbus by including the interviews of particular people that support that argument, by going to places and researching the annuals of history by the writer and by reviewing the scholarly works of others who did the research as well.

So this is really good because Brother Lamont has left a map for our young people to follow and to move forward with our more true history. He shows how and why Africans in Mexico cannot mention their race. They cannot lobby for help as Blacks or Africans because in the early 1800s, signers of the peace in Mexico had to agree to be "Mexicans," not Blacks or Africans by law. They want to leave us out of the history books so that our children can be denied this...

This book will be a contribution to our young people. The covers will be taken off and they will clearly understand that we are the indigenous people on all of the continents of the earth.

And so I just want to thank our brother for his contribution to this effort.

- ***Mfundishi Jhutyms Ka N Heru El-Salim***

Author of the book: *Spiritual Warriors are Healers*

Table of Contents

Foreword i
Introduction 1
Preface 3

An Open Letter:
To Blacks in Cuajiniquilapa, Mexico 5

Chapter One Cuajinicuilapa, Mexico 9

This chapter introduces some of the people who live in and around a small central market village in an area of Mexico that is said to have the largest concentration of African people in the country. It will report some of the challenges Black and Indian people said they face there.

Chapter Two In Search of Freedom 26

This chapter briefly discusses the history of freedom struggles in Mexico and details the marriage between Africans and Indians that helped the once Spanish colony become an independent republic. This overview includes the trials and tribulations of a former slave who rose to help abolish slavery, was named president, and was subsequently run from office and killed by political opponents who wanted to maintain white supremacy in Mexico.

Chapter Three

The Greatest Story Never Told   51

This chapter lays out the significant historical events that have shaped the Americas, specifically, and the world as a whole. It includes references to the experts and scholars who advance the arguments.

A.	Early America	51
B.	Out of Africa	64
C.	Out of Asia	66
D.	Out of Europe	70
E.	Out of Africa II	73
F.	Out of Asia II	76
G.	Out of Europe II	83
H.	Are Black People Victims of Revenge?	88

Chapter Four

The House of God   99

This chapter reviews some of the common themes that are found in stone in ancient Mexico, Central America and Egypt. It will argue, by way of ancient languages and symbols, that the Word of God is good news and guidance for the suffering first family of the earth.

Epilogue   107
Statement of Purpose and Methodology   135

Appendices 161

- A- The Original Americans Were Black Muurs? 163
- B- Indigenous of the World Complain to the UN 171
- C- Black Mexico Is Spreading Wings? 177
- D- Nzingha, Warrior Queen of Nature? 183
- E- Sembene Pictures the Voice of the Ancients 189
- F- The Gullah And Sierra Leone 195
- G- Slavery and Florida Revisited 201
- H- Education for Black New Yorkers? 209
- I- The Toll Paid by Those Who Forge a Way 213
- J- Sidney Poitier Returns to the *Door of No Return* 221
- K- Do Vaccines Cure or Kill? 227
- L- Apocalypto: And the Missing Link 233
- M- Juneteenth 237
- N- A Snapshot of the Theology of the Nation of Islam 241

Illustrations 259

Acknowledgements 263

About the Author 265

Introduction

In the Name of Allah the Beneficent the Merciful

In the *Nation of Islam*, its followers are taught to study all things and hold fast to that which is good. Its leader, The Hon. *Elijah Muhammad* throughout the years has announced to the world that the Blackman is the original man and is "as old as GOD himself."

Some of his followers have taken to *Fact Finding Missions* to verify his teachings. They make great sacrifices, going above and beyond to prove that this *Messenger of Allah* in our midst is sent directly from God, with a profound knowledge and history of what was, what is, and what is going to come about in the future.

Lamont Muhammad is one who has dedicated years of study and research by traveling the earth over, throughout the Middle East, Africa, Mexico, Asia, the Caribbean and the America's, while uncovering many ancient cultures that have been intentionally hidden from the black man and woman, and the world.

As you read on, you will come to learn through his research and own personal experiences just how he brought these truths to light. It is greatly inspiring to witness the confirmation of the truth when it is made manifest.

At one point the author takes us on a journey through the history of the Aztecs and Pyramids of Mexico, (Yes that' right, *Pyramids!*) and has unearthed some of the most profound and advanced cultures from the deepest roots of that nation before cohabitation and race mixing occurred. In his finale, Bro. Muhammad takes the opportunity to marry prophecy and divinity to the purpose of the black family, as he gives a brief chronological summary of the teachings of the Most Honorable Elijah Muhammad and the history of the Nation of Islam in the West under the leadership of the Honorable Minister Louis Farrakhan.

The Bible has it that God would reveal these truths unto babes, making it scripturally prophetic that these truths be told; Hence, the babes are now talking. Let us embrace with much appreciation what we are about to receive on the following pages as we prepare for an enlightened unveiling of history through the eyes of the author....

Raymond Sharrieff Muhammad

Editor-in Chief

Preface

Africa in Mexico is a place called the Costa Chica, according to a Belizean friend who drives up and down Mexico's west coast from Belize, Central America to Los Angeles, and up to Canada often. He challenged me, as a "Black journalist," to visit, talk to, and write about the Black people who live in Cuajinicuilapa, Mexico. In October 1998, I hired a translator in Belize, and set out for Africa in Mexico.

We arrived to meet Black people, including Indians, who do not exist in government, church or other institutional records in Mexico by law. There are no census figures on the descendants of Africa or so-called Indians in Mexico and many complained to me they have been virtually erased from the history their children get in school. The history that is taught in schools there is based on the Spanish conquest. "Blacks were slaves" and the "Indians were defeated," they complained.

I knew that story. I am a product of the New York City public school system. I wanted to share the other history lessons I learned outside of the official classroom, so I pledged to some of the people I met there that I would write newspaper articles about them in the United States (US) and, later, a brief, footnoted overview of Black/Indian history in Mexico. I also pledged to include a reason for our treatment in the the Americas and the world, based on the Theology of the Nation of Islam (NOI). They would, we agreed, later determine what needed to be translated into Spanish for their children.

When I began to research I discovered Africans had previously been revered as gods by some in Mexico and the rest of the Americas, that they may have been here before the so-called Indians, and that Africans have historically fought alongside indigenous and other people to establish independent republics in the west. I was shocked to learn, I must confess, that the battle for the Alamo was fought over slavery. I was never taught in school that Texas was a state in Mexico until Mexico abolished slavery. That is when the Lone Star State seceded from Mexico, plotted to be annexed by the US-where slavery was still lawful. I did not know that General Ulysses S. Grant, blamed the bloodiest war in United States history on the fact that the United States took half of Mexico and expanded slavery into much of the new territory. The move angered the abolitionists, which brought on the Civil War, Gen. Grant suggested in his autobiography.

Finally, I learned the condition of most Black people in the Americas and the world is a reflection of a determined idea of White people to replace Blacks. What started out as my gift to the people I had met in Mexico became a new education for me of what I thought I had already come to know.

[Monolithic Head   Height 5' 4" San Lorenzo, Vera Cruz (1000 – 300 B.C.)]

An Open Letter to the People of Cuajinicuilapa, Mexico

Greetings!
In the Name of the Creator of the Seen and Unseen, I greet the people of Cuajinicuilapa, Mexico, in Peace!

I pray this message finds you in good health and moving forward…

In October, 1998, a little over 17 years ago, I told Mrs. Hortencia Zapata Bacho, Gabriel Loya, Rosa Marie Martinez A., Azucena Dominuez Martinez, Natividad Silva Hernandez, Marcelino Dominuez C., and a few others – that I would write some of your story for communities I knew back in Belize, Central America, and in the United States. I said I would give you back some of the missing pages of Black history in Mexico, and the world for you and your children. More importantly, in my opinion, as I said then, I would explain the actions of others through the teachings of the Honorable Elijah Muhammad (THEM), which would tell you why your history has been erased from the history books there and elsewhere.

This new edition of this project is the fulfillment of that humble pledge.

Let me first begin by thanking Mr. Loya, the director of the Cultural Institute in Cuajinicuilapa at that time, for reading from the book *The Black Population of Mexico*, by the late (University of Veracruz) Professor Gonzalo Aquirre Beltran. When I heard him read that there were 250,000 Black people living in the Costa Chica (Southwestern Mexico) before the enslaved trade began in the Americas, I heard exactly the kind of information I was looking for there. The book confirmed that Black people were in Mexico before "Columbus discovered America," and confirmed the words of THEM who said, paraphrasing: Everywhere the explorer has gone, he (or she) has discovered that we had already been there." This project will show those words to be true.

Black Mexico: The Greatest Story Never Told (Black Mexico) is a footnoted picture of the waves of Black people who migrated to the Americas from "Africa." Black people not only "discovered" it, civilized it, and developed it, but eventually fell victim to a new people. The new people have claimed the Americas as their own and have led a determined campaign to erase any evidence that we were here first.

Finally, when I thought my research was complete and I was wrapping up this project in late 2012 or early 2013, I got a call from a friend in Baltimore.

"Lamont, don't close out your book until you read *When Rocks Cry Out*, by Horace Butler."

I have since read the book a number of times and found Mr. Butler's research, although doubted by some, provides the answers to many questions I had in my head and helped to raise a few more. The book goes straight to the issue of why Blacks are ignored in modern history books. I believe it to be an important contribution to the debate and I too would suggest that serious students read it and other works that are mentioned in this project.

The appendices in this edition are selected articles that were written on related subjects I thought some might appreciate there and here in the US.

I pray you in the Costa Chica, the folks with whom I discussed this project in Belize, and folks elsewhere, find a benefit in this labor. I merely ask that you hold on to what you believe to be true, and save the rest for later...

All praise belongs to Allah, The Lord of All Worlds. The mistakes are mine.

Bro. Lamont
Febuary 24, 2016
Mount Vernon, New York

Chapter One

CUAJINICUILAPA, MEXICO

[Mrs. Hortencia Zapata Bacho (r), owner of Ocaso Restaurant, 1998. Photo credit: Lamont Muhammad.]

You would think you were in Africa from the etched Black faces, tall coconut trees, thatched roof houses and the flowers that dot the South Pacific coast of Mexico in the Costa Chica (short coast). Estimates, of the total Black population of Mexico range from 600,000 to many millions. Most live in the states of Veracruz, along the Mexican Gulf coast; and in Guerrero and Oaxaca (pronounced: Wa-ha-ka) on the Pacific coast.

[Note: The town of Yanga, in the state of Veracruz, "has received considerable attention as one of America's oldest 'maroon communities': settlements founded by fugitive slaves."[1] The town is named for the Nigerian Muslim who resisted slavery for decades and finally "negotiated with the Spaniards to establish a free black community" there in 1609.[2] The state is also known for Olmec Heads and is described as the main region for that ancient civilization (1122 B.C.). Interestingly, Olmec outposts have been identified here in the Costa Chica, which will be examined later.]

The Costa Chica is a 200-mile long coastal region that begins just southeast of Acapulco, Guerrero, and ends in Puerto Angel, Oaxaca; two of the three poorest states in Mexico. The third, Chiapas, the most southern, is where the Maya and government forces continue a protracted war over control of the land. The Costa Chica, however, is said to have the heaviest concentration of Black people in Mexico. I was told the central market village of Cuajinicuilapa (pronounced: Kwa-he-ni-kwi-lapa), was a good place to get started on the story of Blacks in Mexico.

---

[1] *Africa's Legacy in Mexico* www.smithsondianeducation.org, "What is a Mexican," by Miriam Jimenez Roman, 05.15.08.
[2] Ibid., p 1

Cuajinicuilapa was a four hour bus ride south of Acapulco, along route #200. It did not take long for my translator and I to realize that October is the beginning of the rainy season there. We crossed over many swollen rivers that rushed down the Sierra Madre mountains and on out to the Pacific Ocean.

When we arrived at Cuajinicuilapa, we found an air-conditioned hotel and dropped our bags. Our next stop was the police station to declare our intention to do a feature story on Black people in the area. My mission, I explained, was to determine how many people in the area considered themselves descendants of slaves and how many trace their origins to pre-Columbus African traders, who, evidence shows, set up settlements and missions there before Christopher Columbus was born. This will be further discussed later.

Two Black men who said they were the highest ranking officers on the police force, the director of public security, Commander Rufino Quiterio Urban, 55, and 2nd Commander Tomas Pena Salinas, 34, who called us cousins. Commander Urban, in a T-Shirt, was a barrel-chested but humble soldier with a big pistol on his hip. He described his town as a peaceful and friendly place with a population of half African-Mexican and half Indigenous-Mexican, including a small percentage of Mestizo (mixed with white). He said other villages along the Costa Chica were as much as 80 percent African-Mexican, through translator

Adam Muhammad. But the specific demographics do not exist on paper in Mexico, by law, I learned later.

Officer Salinas said Blacks, mostly farmers and fishermen here, came to this part of Mexico as slaves in the hulls of ships. He had no knowledge to contribute to the pre-colonial African presence in Mexico. He said he was taught that Blacks were slaves, were freed and pretty much stayed "where we got off the ships." In time the Indians accepted the Africans, he said with a smile, and now we are melting into one people.

Both officers described Blacks here as poor and simple people who are living a good life but eluded to a mental and spiritual damage that has been done to dark skin people in a world of white supremacy. They directed us to a Cultural Institute across the street from the police station that was designed to instill a sense of pride in young African/Indigenous people. It would not be open until after school, they explained.

During our conversation with the officers we noticed that there were truckloads of other officers zipping up and down the main street and checking in with the station. Commander Urban explained that the soldiers were on patrol in the surrounding areas. We could not but help notice that this part of Mexico was an armed camp. Our bus was stopped and inspected by armed and ready soldiers on our way to this armed camp. We later learned that there were guerrilla soldiers in the mountains who were maintaining an over 500-year resistance to the European invasion. We knew of the widely reported conflicts in the mountains and villages of Chiapas but did not know that there were insurgents in all three southern states. The soldiers we saw were a modern day version of the Buffalo Soldiers of American west fame. It was another case of brother hunting down and killing brother in a war that was began by an invader. One brother is still fighting to get his land back from the historical enemy of both and the other brother needs a job. This subject will be further discussed later.

Next we were directed to the Ocaso Restaurant, which happened to be next door to our hotel. The owner, Mrs. Hortencia Zapata Bacho, a beautiful African-Mexican grandmother, greeted us warmly and fed us like kings. When she learned of our purpose for being in her village she sat with us and mapped out the appropriate places we needed to examine, including the Cultural Institute. She told us that her son is a teacher here, and that he helps to sponsor a Black convention in Oaxaca each March. The Convention of Black Villages was established to link the 24 African-Mexican villages in the Costa Chica, she explained. These villages were scattered around the Costa Chica, in the Mountainous and hilly coastal areas of Guerrero and Oaxaca.

Across the street from the restaurant was a pharmacy in which we met Sonia Salina, 20, an attractive African/Indian cashier who was upbeat about life there and was happy to be interviewed as a representative of her very special people, as she described them.

She did not have any historical knowledge of Black folk's contributions to Mexico because, she said, she had never been taught the subject. Discrimination based on color does exist there but she did not feel affected by it, because Blacks are the majority in Cuajinicuilapa, and operate on all levels here. Some dark skinned people here wish they were lighter, yes, but not me." I believe our color makes us "the most beautiful," Ms. Salina proudly declared.

When night fell on Cuajinicuilapa, the police patrols slowed down to an occasional snail's pace along the sparsely crowded, dimly lit main strip.

A few blocks up from the hotel we discovered a business in the making. Rosa Marie Martinez A., her daughter Azucena Dominuez Martinez, 15, and niece Natividad Silva Hernandez, 16, were comfortably lounging outside a shop that was dotted with mounds of sand. The owners were expanding their restaurant and home. Inside the small cement box, construction equipment surrounded a horizontal refrigerator that was stacked with beers and sodas. When we told them why we were there they found chairs and invited us to sit down outside to talk with them. When we pulled out

[Azucena D. Martinez, 15, did not think she was worthy of being photographed, 1998. Photo credit: Lamont Muhammad]

our cameras we were surprised. "No! Don't take my picture. I am too ugly," said pretty Azucena. She said she was not worthy of being photographed, but finally agreed to give us a cautious grin the next day. Interestingly, Azucena, who we were told is an exceptional student in school, considered herself ugly because she is dark, but saw her cousin Natividad as pretty, despite the fact that she is of an even darker hue. Azucena, who practiced her English on us, was an example of a beautiful young woman who considered herself unattractive, because of social pressures here.

Marcelino Dominuez C., his wife Rosa Maria Martinez A., (standing) and niece Natividad Silva Hernandez, 1998. Photo credit: Lamont Muhammad.]

Brother Adam, the translator, was born to an African-Belizean father and an Indigenous-Guatemalan mother. He has lived in Belize and Guatemala. The extensive traveler had also lived in Mexico. He said Africans and Indians often avoided the sun throughout the region for fear their skin is dark enough. Some people here do

[Translator and guide, Adam B. Muhammad back in Belize, 1998. Photo credit: Lamont Muhammad.]

measure beauty by color, he explained to me in English, and to them in Spanish for conformation.

The three agreed with him, but said they did not run from the sun. They knew people, however, who do. Yet, all agreed, despite the social pressure to avoid dark skin, the two dark skin people have a natural affinity for each other. "(The) Larasas, Negros and the Larasas, Indios (Black people and Indian people)" are becoming one, Mrs. Martinez said.

When we asked what they knew about their history Martinez shrugged. She too complained that the history of Black people was not being taught in school.

"All I know is that a slave ship wrecked and people came ashore and stayed. That's what I was taught and that's how they keep us down. Even when they teach us the Bible they leave out the parts that are important to us because they want to continue to oppress us. They (whites) know we are a great people but they need somebody to look down on," she explained.

Martinez, originally from Acapulco, had no complaints about her little community. She said many African/Indians do have a stake in the economy here but most "just have jobs." Her husband,

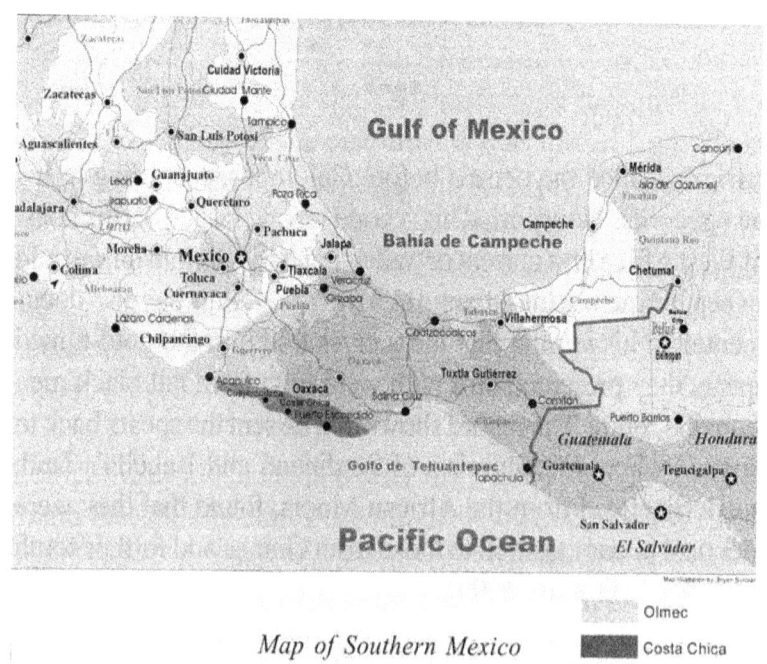

Map of Southern Mexico

Marcelino Dominuez drives taxi to Acapulco each day picking up rides along the way. He is for hire around the big city during the day and picks up rides on his way home evenings. He apparently was the engine behind the restaurant his wife runs. He showed up just before we left. He was quiet, maybe suspicious, but cordial. He offered his services to get us back to Acapulco when we were ready but the bus was far more affordable.

As we rose from our chairs Martinez called out to a passing cyclist. It was the director of the Cultural Institute, Gabriel Loya, 29, on his way home. The center was not opened that day because he was required to attend a special program in the area, he explained. We scheduled a meeting for the morning.

****

After a morning stroll around the busy market hub with cameras in hand, we sat down with Mr. Loya in the town center. He was carrying, in Spanish, a book entitled: *The Black Population of Mexico*, by the late Gonzalo Aquirre Beltran, former professor at the University of Veracruz. The premise of the book, which was published in 1946, is that African culture is "the third (or hidden) root of the Americas." There is a Spanish root, an Indigenous root and an omitted African root from Mexican history, the book argued. Professor Beltran said that there were as many as 250,000 Africans in this region before the Europeans discovered the west and began the Trans-Atlantic slave-trade.

Professor Beltran (January 20, 1908-1996) was an anthropologist who focused his studies on African-Mexican studies. The author of other books and many articles also served as the director of the National Indian Institute and as Assistant Secretary for Popular Culture and Extra Curricular Education.[3]

Africans outnumbered the Spanish in Mexico during the colonial period, the professor explained in his book. He also noted the arrival of Bantu language speaking Sudanese people here as late as 1910, in the book.

Loya said Beltran's work was not available to him in school. He, like the others we talked to here, was taught to trace their roots to a shipwreck that can still be seen off the nearby coast of Maldonado during low tide, he said. "If it is not about Spanish culture we don't get it in school. The history we thirst for has been written out of the record. Dark skin in this society represents ignorance, poverty, criminality and otherwise worthlessness. There are no positive references to Black people," he complained. "My father told me to marry a White (Indian) girl because it would be better for my children. I did and I love my wife, but I know we have to stop thinking that way.

---

[3]*Gonzalo Aquirre Beltran*, wikipedia.org, 05.15.08

[Children in Cuajinicuilapa perform "Dance of the Devil." Mr. Loya is pictured on the far right, 1998. Photo credit: Lamont Muhammad]

Loya said he is teaching traditional dance at his center. He uses dance, he said to work on the way young people think about themselves and their ancestors. A popular cultural dance, complete with African drums is the "Dance of the Diablos," the Devil Dance. It could have easily been called the stomp dance, but Loya didn't know if the dance symbolized the Devil stomping the ancestors or the children of the ancestors stomping the Devil.

"No one knows what it means," he said. Loya is also a part of a broader cultural movement that he said was started by a Trinidadian Padre who has been working in the Costa Chica since 1984. We were disappointed to learn that we could not travel to meet Padre Glen

Jemmott, 53, because a Pacific coast hurricane had preceded us by a few days and made the roads impassable. We went to the library instead.

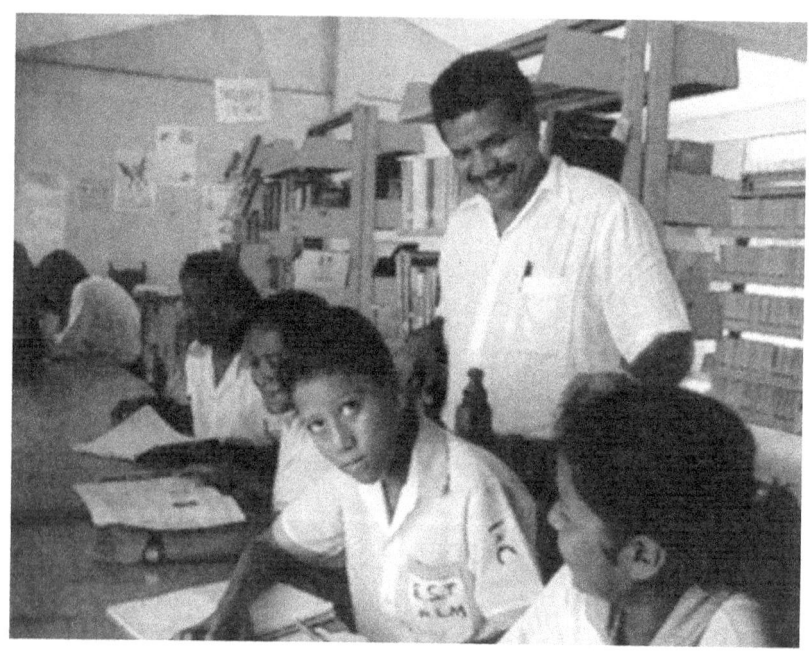

[*Julio Agustiniano and students at the municipal library in Cuajinicuilapa, 1998. Photo credit: Lamont Muhammad*]

Julio Agustiniano, 47, the municipal librarian here, was the first person we met in Cuajinicuilapa who was familiar with an African oral tradition that predated the slave ships. He said he grew up in an African styled village with African thatched roofs and traditional healers. "Africans came to Mexico with the culture of the Moors to trade with the Indians. They set up trading posts on the coast. The Indians lived in the hills. Eventually, after trading and building trust, they began to take wives from the Indigenous communities.

The Africans taught the Indians how to build better homes, etc.," he explained. The story was related to him when he was a child. He said he has never read it.

Mr. Agustiniano had no complaints about racism in Mexico but said he understood the struggle. "These (White) people only promote themselves. We have to learn to excel and promote ourselves," although he admitted he has to walk a tight line when it comes to what books he can order and promote at the library.

As we left the library we heard a loud burst of fireworks. "What's the occasion?" We asked Loya. "People do it all the time," he replied, "especially when someone kidnaps a woman. You know, like when somebody loses a wife?" He was smiling.

Later at dinner we met a teacher who said he had four years experience teaching in public schools in the United States but was extremely frustrated teaching in Cuajinicuilapa. Professor Jorge Andrue Zapata, Bacho's son, said he was frustrated with a curriculum that promotes European culture and White people as the ultimate plateau.

"In Mexico, blond hair and blue eyes are perfect. How do you change that?" He asked.

Mr. Zapata, like Agustiniano, complained that he had been prohibited from introducing new subjects or books to his students in the classroom without written approval from Mexico City. He said he is a part of the consciousness movement outside the formal classroom. He too works with Padre Glyn.

After the 1997 "Convention of Black Villages," Lula Sutherland, writing for the on-line journal, *The Black World Today*, interviewed Padre Glyn. He told the reporter that he was invited to a teenage parishioner's birthday dinner right after he conducted his first mass in Oaxaca. A drunk, dinner guest started feeling his kinky hair and said it was impossible for him to be the new parson because Blacks were not good enough to hold such a high position.

"He said we (Blacks) are a common people, ordinary, we can't aim that high," the Padre recalled the man saying. Soon he came to learn that most of the people in the surrounding 24 (African-Mexican) villages viewed themselves the same way. By 1991, he said, he and other organizers began planning efforts designed to address the need for Black (and Indigenous) Mexicans to accept themselves as individuals who are not only valuable today, but were vital yesterday in the forging of modern Mexico. Organizers established the month of March for the Black villages convention. It is an annual event that is held in Oaxaca.[4] Because of a storm in the south, we were advised to return to a hurricane that was threatening Belize at the time.

---

[4]*The Black World Today* < www.tbwt.org > "Black Mexico," Lula Strickland, /The Series/Part 4, 1997

Black Mexico: The Greatest Story Never Told

Faces of Cuajiniquilapa -All photos by Lamont Muhammad, except top left, by Adam Muhammad

Chapter Two

IN SEARCH OF FREEDOM

[Commander Rufino Quiterio Urban (l) and 2nd Commander Tomas Pena Salinas, 1998. Photo credit: Lamont Muhammad.]

In order to discuss the history of the Mexican Republic we must begin with the events of 1810 that led to the first revolt against Mexico's first colonial ruler, the Spanish Crown. It started when soldiers for the Crown cut down grapevines belonging to a Spanish Priest who wanted to grow grapes and make his own wine. At the time, the Crown required Spanish subjects to buy wine manufactured and bottled in Spain. Padre Miguel Hidalgo was a White priest whom the locals respected as a faithful man. When the colonial authorities destroyed his grapevines, the priest issued a declaration of Independence from colonial Spain. He called on all Mexicans to stand up and declare Mexico an independent republic. History shows that the Africans and Indians, the bottom of the food chain in Mexico, responded to Padre Hidalgo by waging war against Europeans there, killing all they could find.

"They immediately began to kill and pillage. They exacted revenge against White people for the condition of servitude they suffered so long," said Muhammad Abdullah Muhammad, the Dominican born, former Latino Minister of the Nation of Islam, and student of history. "These mob attacks surprised Padre Hidalgo. He had not planned the rebellions, nor was he able to control the freedom fighters. Mr. Hidalgo was eventually captured. He recanted his call to arms before he was executed in 1811, but it was too late. The race war had begun," the New York based scholar said.

After Hidalgo was executed, Padre Jon Maria Morelos Y Pavon, a brown skinned man, according to Min. Muhammad, assumed a military general's position over the revolutionary army. In 1813 he convened the Congress of Chilpancingo and called for the abolition of slavery and tribute. But, unlike the masses that rose up to kill Whites, Padre Pavon did not harbor hatred for them. In fact, Muhammad said, he referred to White people as the "inheritors of the kingdom," and argued that many Whites hated the Spanish also. Pavon not only wanted to spare the lives of White people in Mexico, according to Muhammad. He argued they should lead the new republic and ordered "killed," all rebel leaders plotting to drive White people out of Mexico. Pavon was nevertheless, captured and executed in 1815, by Crown loyalists.

The execution almost killed the revolution in Mexico. The fathers of the revolution were dead, in jail or again working for the Spanish Crown, except for one man. He was an ex-slave who led "a little body of unconquered men" throughout "the darkest hours of the long revolution."[5] General Vincente Guerrero, for whom the state of Guerrero was named, was field commissioned Captain by Hidalgo during Guerrero's first battle against the Spanish Army. He is described as African-Indian. He rose to the rank of General quickly, distinguishing himself as a brave and skillful warrior. At a point during the war, the Crown sent Guerrero's father Pedro, a loyalist, to offer him land and wealth if he would stop the rebellion. Guerrero, however, "pledged himself no rest until the hated Spaniard had been driven in the sea."[6]

Guerrero defeated Spain's most decorated general in battle twice. But General Augustine de Iturbide, himself secretly planning to revolt against Spain and claim Mexico for himself, offered Guerrero a deal. He

---

[5] J.A. Rogers, *World's Great Men of Color, Vol. II*, 1947, page 183
[6] Ibid., p.183

promised to revolt against the Crown if Guerrero would support him. Guerrero agreed. The combined forces defeated General Santa Ana and the power in Mexico shifted into the hands of the revolutionaries.

In truth, the 1821 victory of Iturbide and Guerrero was accomplished while Spain was under occupation by the French army of Napoleon.[7] Spain officially lost Mexico and the rest of her colonies in the Americas in 1821. But the revolution so many fought and died for never freed the landless poor from oppression. What began as a social revolution was co-opted by the rich, who used the opportunity to consolidate their position and to establish a reactionary independence from Spain.[8] Guerrero was forced to realize the hard way, that the rich had no plan to improve the condition of poor people in Mexico.

The first mistake Guerrero and his supporters made was at the independence agreement of 1821. The faustian pact at the Independence Plan of Iguala abolished slavery and tribute. But in return, however, the freedom fighters had to agree to no preferences for Africans or Indians. The agreement made it illegal for a member of Congress to mention the race of an individual on the floor of that chamber. All government and church records were prohibited from identifying people by race. That is why there are no official counts of Africans or Indians in Mexico today.

---

[7] Universal Standard Encyclopedia, 1956, Vol.16 p.5711
[8] Universal Standard, p.5711

Everybody is counted as Mexican,⁹ as it was agreed then.

In 1822, Iturbide crowned himself Emperor of Mexico, and the poor continued to suffer. He was pressured to abdicate the throne on March 19, of the following year, was ridiculed and eventually exiled."¹⁰

Guadalupe Victoria (Felix Fernandez) was named president of Mexico in 1824, but raging battles continued behind the scenes of the new government over the redistribution of lands formerly controlled by the Spanish Crown. The renowned historian Joel A. Rogers, author of *Worlds Great Men of Color*, described the internal war as a battle between Freemasons – the Scottish Rite and the York Rite masons. The former, mostly white, wanted to keep control of the lands in the hands of the rich.

Since 1821, the record shows that politics in Mexico has amounted to a pendulum swing between advocates for the rich and for the poor. Rogers said Guerrero was handed the government and named President of Mexico in 1825. Other records say he became president in 1829.

> *Guerrero at once set about improving the conditions of the masses, composed of*

---

⁹ Ted Vincent, The Daily Challenge, "Afro-Mexicans Who Fused National Identity," June 12 – 14, 1998 p.5

¹⁰ Enrique Krauze, *Mexico: Biography of Power*, Harpers Collins Publishers, 1997, p. 128

Indians, half-breeds, and Negroes. He ordered schools to be built, established free libraries – reading had been forbidden – proclaimed religious liberty, established a coinage system, suspended the death penalty, and took other steps far in advance of his time. His most important act was the abolishment of slavery. Though inspired by the Constitution of the United States, he went further than that document. He ordered the immediate release of every slave in Mexico. The estimated number of Negro slaves was 10,595 blacks and 1059 mulattoes, with Guerrero's native state containing the largest number. The remainder were Indians and half-breeds, some of whom had a Negro strain.

The Mexican constitution, which is as liberal a document as has ever been penned, was much the work of Guerrero. One of its clauses read, "All inhabitants, whether White, African, or Indian, are qualified to hold office."

Guerrero's emancipation proclamation was put into effect almost without resistance because it did not entail great economic loss to the rich, except in one state, namely Texas.

> *The Texans were chiefly Americans who had migrated into Mexico with their slaves to escape anti slavery agitation in the United States. They made it clear that they would not give up their slaves without a struggle and Guerrero, who was busy fighting his enemies in Mexico City, was forced to leave them alone.* [11]

President Guerrero's enemies, however, drove him from his Presidential Palace and back to the mountains from which he once waged war on the Crown. He, again, defeated every force sent against him for four years, until a Captain he trusted lured him down from the mountains and onto his ship. Guerrero was subsequently arrested and killed after a mock trial.[12]

> *They could not bear the sight of one of Guerrero's race occupying the presidential chair and ruthlessly destroyed a government whose only faults were excessive clemency and liberalism, a Mexican historian wrote.*[13]

Mexico exploded in mass pandemonium when news spread that the President had been killed. The new President, the former General Carlos Maria de Bustamante, was forced to flee the country.

---

[11] Ibid., p. 184
[12] Ibid., p. 185
[13] Ibid., p.185

Captain Picaluga, the other conspirator, was executed. Guerrero's wife was eventually paid a pension, honors were conferred on members of his family and cities and a state were named in his honor.[14]

Of course, it was difficult to cross reference the chronology Rogers provided. In fact, in the chronology provided by Enrique Krauze, in his book, *Mexico: Biography of Power*, President Guerrero is not even mentioned. The chronology begins in 1325, with the founding of what became Mexico City, by the Aztecs. Interestingly, the Aztecs admitted they found pyramids when they arrived in the Valley of Mexico that were "built by (Black people) the 'Gods.'"[15]

Mr. Krauze continues with other events leading up to 1824, the year Mexico officially became a republic. Then it jumps to 1833, when Santa Ana, the former Spanish general Guerrero and Iturbide combined forces to defeat in 1821, was elected President of Mexico on the Conservative-Liberal ticket (May 16, 1833).[16]

But politics in Mexico continued to be so volatile that Santa Ana was defeated and reelected three times by the following April of 1834, in a continuing battle between the Conservatives and the Liberals in Mexico. On March 2, 1836, the same day Jose Justo Corro was elected president of Mexico, Texas, mostly driven by

---

[14] Ibid, p 185
[15] Paul Alfred Barton, *A History of the African-Olmecs*, 1st Books Library, 2001, p. 102
[16] Wikipedia, *List of Presidents of Mexico*, on-line, 03.22.07

slavery expansionists from the U.S., declared itself the "Lone Star Republic," and independent of Mexico.

To his credit, Santa Ana, who had previously defended slavery for the Crown, marched his army to the gates of the famous Alamo and defeated the pro-slavery rebels led by William B. Travis, Jim Bowie and Davy Crockett. The Alamo fell on March 6, 1836. The few survivors included a few women and children, and a slave named Joe, who had belonged to Travis.[17] Santa Ana "gave them blankets and money and told them to go out and spread the word that anyone who opposed him would meet the same fate as the defenders of the Alamo.[18]

The Alamo defenders included 30 men from Tennessee; 15, from Kentucky; 14, from Pennsylvania; 13, from Virginia; 11, from Texas; seven, from North Carolina, Missouri and South Carolina; six, from New York; four, from Georgia, Louisiana, Massachusetts and Ohio; three, from Mississippi; two, from Arkansas and Alabama; one, came from the states of Connecticut, Illinois, New Hampshire, New Jersey, Rhode Island and Vermont, and one was born in Alabama or Kentucky.

Eleven were from England; nine, from Ireland; four, from Scotland; two, from Denmark and Germany; one from Wales; and one was born in England or Ireland.

---

[17]Stephan Ortman, *The Alamo*, Casa Editrice Bonechi, Florece, Italy, 2007, p. 23
[18]Ibid, p. 23

There were 18 Alamo defenders whose places of birth were unknown. Among those who died at the Alamo was one freed Black man named John.[19]

Most of the Texans had moved to Mexico from the U.S. believing slavery would be abolished in the U.S. first. In fact, slavery was abolished in Mexico 44-years before the institution of slavery was abolished in the United States of America.

One month and two weeks after the fall of the Alamo, however, under the battle cry: "Remember the Alamo," General Sam Houston defeated Santa Ana at the battle of San Jacinto, Mexico (April 21, 1836, near today's Houston, Texas). The defeat of the Mexicans meant slavery was maintained in the new "Lone Star Republic," but Mexico did not submit to the setback.

> *Even after the loss of Texas, Mexican officials refused to formally acknowledge Texas independence on the grounds that it "would be equivalent to the sanction and recognition of slavery." After Texas independence the slave population mushroomed and the number of runaways across the South Texas-North Mexico border, increased. In 1842 Mexico's Constitutional Congress reasserted the nation's commitment to fugitive slaves. In*

---

[19]Ibid.,p. 27

1847, 38,753 slaves and 102,961 whites were listed in the first official Texas census.

In 1850, in a new treaty accord with the United States, Mexico again refused to provide for the return of fugitive slaves. The slave institution in Texas was continuously undermined by defiant Tejanos (Mexicans in Texas) who took great risks and invested enormous resources toward facilitating the escape of enslaved Africans. The Texas to Mexico routes to freedom constituted major unacknowledged extensions of the "Underground Railroad." Tejanos were variously accused of "tampering with slave property," "consorting with blacks" and stirring up among the slave population "a spirit of insubordination."[20]

The U.S. annexed Texas in 1845, which kicked off the Mexican War (1846 – 1848). At one point U.S. troops even occupied the capital, Mexico City.

On September 16, 1847 – the anniversary of Mexico's independence – the troops of General Winfield Scott had raised the

---

[20] Ron Wilkins, *Mexico's Legacy: A Refuge for Fugitive Slaves and Black Job-Seekers New Perspectives on the Immigration Debate*, www.blackcommentator.com, May, 4, 2006 – Issue 182

Stars and Stripes over the National Palace. Nothing could erase this insult from the collective Mexican memory. A year later, when the fever for gold flared up in California, Mexico had to surrender the richest, though almost uninhabited half of that territory to the United States. Nor would the discord end there. Within a short time, Mexico lost another stretch of land along its northern border, and in 1859, at the height of the Guerra de Reforma ("War of the Reform?) between liberals and Conservatives, Juarez's Liberal government was on the point of accepting the proposals of President Buchanan, under which Mexico would virtually become a protectorate of the United States, in exchange for the economic and military aid against the Conservatives. This project for economic expansion – actually articulated in a formal treaty – fell through because of several unexpected happenings, among them a veto by the United States Senate and the outbreak of the American Civil War.[21]

Before the Mexican-American War, "Mexico's territory included what are now California, Nevada, Utah, Arizona, New Mexico, most of Colorado, and parts of

---

[21] Krauze, 1997, p. 5

Kansas, Oklahoma, and Wyoming."[22] The territory of the United States grew by 500,000 square miles.[23] At the time, the governor of California, the richest state in Mexico, was a descendant of Africans, Governor Pio Pico.

> *The Pico family was among the first settlers of the little town that today is the metropolis of Los Angeles. Those original settlers came from central Mexico and Sonora, and the majority of them had African heritage, according to 1790s census records.*[24]

"Anglo-Americans" raided California. They stole horses from the Californians and declared the richest territory in Mexico a separate "Bear Flag Republic."[25]

Governor Pico and his brother Andres are credited with vigorously resisting the annexing of California. The family owned a great portion of what is now Los Angeles County, but Pio Pico died a poor man. He was swindled out of his wealth, exploited and conquered by the Anglo-Americans.

The U.S. netted 80 percent of Mexico's mineral wealth when it took "half" of the nation in 1848, according to

---

[22] Wim Coleman, *The Mexican War*, Discovery Enterprises, Ltd, Carlisle, MA, 1998, p.6
[23] Ibid., p. 7
[24] Online: members.aol.com/_ht_a/fsln/gallery/pico1. 6.14.2006
[25] Howard Zinn, A People's History of the United States, 2003, p. 168

Professor Ron Wilkins of California State University. If California and Texas were still a part of Mexico, he said, Mexico would have more oil than Saudi Arabia.[26]

The Mexican-American War was mainly fought to expand slavery in the U.S. The following excerpt from an editorial that ran in a Manchester, New Hampshire newspaper makes the point.

> *We have heretofore held our peace in regard to the annexation of Texas, for the purpose of seeing whether our Nation would attempt so base an action. We call it base, because it would be giving men that live upon the blood of others, an opportunity of dipping their hand still deeper in the sin of slavery....Have we not enough now?* [27]

Another reason the U.S. moved against Mexico was to take advantage of the political wars waging inside the country between the Conservatives and the Liberals, and the race wars that were raging in the southern stretches of Mexico.

In 1846, the year the Mexican-American War started, the Maya, rose up to annex the Yucatan Peninsula from Mexico.

---

[26] Wilkins, 2006
[27] Zinn, 2003, p. 159

> *We poor Indians are aware of what the whites are doing to injure us, of how many evils they commit against us, even to our children and harmless women. So much injury without basis seems to us a crime. Indeed, therefore, if the Indians revolt, it is because the whites gave them reason; because they have burned the cornfields. They have given just cause for reprisals of the Indians, whom they themselves have killed... They will have to say whether God gave them permission to slaughter us all and that we have no will in the matter... Therefore, if we die at the hands of the whites, patience. The whites think that these things are all ended, but never. It is written in the book of Chilam Balam, and so even has said Jesus Christ, our Lord on earth and beyond, that if the whites will become peaceful, so shall we become peaceful.*[28]

The Maya, from the frontier began to attack the whites with a vengeance. But the Huits, however, "long familiar with the whipping post and peonage, not only failed to rise (to fight) but actually joined the white men against their own race," wrote Nelson Reed, author of *The Caste War of Yucatan*. The Huits were field hands in Western Yucatan. Half the

---

[28] Nelson Reed, *The Caste War of Yucatan*, Stanford University Press, 1964, ps. 46-49

population of the Yucatan was killed or driven out between 1846 and 1850. Thousands were driven into British Honduras or modern day Belize, said Robert Leslie, editor of *A History of Belize*.

"We have (black and brown) populations in Corozal and Orange Walk (northern districts) who live the culture of Mexico. They do not identify with the British Commonwealth at all," Mr. Leslie told me in Belize (1997).

There is no record of the number of Blacks or Indians who sought refuge in British Honduras (Belize). We do know that British Honduras historically provided sanctuary for Mexicans fleeing oppression in Mexico, and visa versa, but not out of any form of sympathy. Both countries practiced an ungodly pigmentocricy with White on top, mixed-race on the second level, and Blacks and Indians on the bottom. Both competed for the land, as opposed to offering help to the victims of invasion and exploitation. But the United States proved to be the biggest winner in the land acquisition game. According to the cartographer who showed Santa Ana the new map of Mexico in 1853, when he was elected president for the eleventh and last time, Santa Ana "burst into tears" when he saw how much of Mexico had been lost to the U.S.[29] But the United States did not avoid repercussions for taking half of Mexico from the new republic. In fact, Civil War

---

[29] Coleman, 1998, p. 63

icon, General Ulysses S Grant suggested that the Mexican War, which was initiated by the U.S., further divided the United States between slave states and non-slave states and "made our greatest national tragedy inevitable."[30] In his autobiography, Gen. Grant said the Mexican-American War was "one of the most unjust ever waged by a stronger against a weaker nation."

> *To us it was an empire and of incalculable value; but it might have been obtained by other means. The Southern rebellion was largely the outgrowth of the Mexican War. Nations, like individuals, are punished for their transgressions. We got our punishment in the most sanguinary and expensive war in modern times.*[31]

When the U.S. finally ended chattel slavery in 1865, some people described the move as a profit making adjustment. Slavery required owners of slaves to buy, house, feed and clothe entire families. But northern industrialists realized the potential for making more money in a market economy. They would pay low or slave wages to workers who were required to feed, clothe and house their families themselves.

Related adjustments were made in Mexico. When the Civil War ended the power hungry shifted strategies in

---

[30] Ibid., p.8
[31] Ibid, p. 8

Mexico from military invasions of the new republic to financial investments, according to Enrique Krauze. In his book, he argues that money was used as a weapon to control human and natural resources in Mexico after the war. By 1910, U.S. investors controlled 38 percent of Mexico's foreign investment in mining, railroads, banking, the oil industry, and agriculture.[32] The former slaves in the U.S. were subjected to like adjustments. The literate and illiterate (teaching slaves to read in the U.S. was illegal during slavery) were challenged by economic destabilization schemes. Self-employed and skilled Blacks, however, were the special targets of the white supremacists.

> *After the Civil War Blacks dominated the skilled trades, particularly in the South. Labor unions were established to force Blacks out of these trades in favor of white immigrants. This era was called the Age of Gompers after the American Federation of Labor (A.F.L.) leader Samuel Gompers. A Jewish immigrant from England, Gompers credits his success to his early training in Hebrew and Talmudic studies at the Jewish Free School in London.*
>
> *Gompers' A.F.L. refused admittance of Blacks and successfully threw thousands out of work. Gompers promoted and encouraged this racial terrorism by his*

---
[32] Krauze, 1997, p. 6

> *white union and actually blamed Blacks for being "strikebreakers," whom he threatened with "a race hatred far worse than ever known." In his public addresses he referred to Blacks as "darkies" and as "superstitious, dull, ignorant, happy-go-lucky, improvident, lazy and, immoral." According to his biographer, Gompers molded the A.F.L. into a true Aryan institution that would affect race and labor relations for more than a century.[33]*

Seventy percent of the Blacks who were lynched in the U.S. during Jim Crow were self-employed, Randall Robinson, author of *The Debt,* told an audience at Kean University in New Jersey in 2000. Many whites, especially the new European arrivals, who were competing for work, seemed to especially detest the sight of progressive Black people. Tyler Anbinder painted a graphic picture of what Black New Yorkers were going through during and after the Civil War in his book *Five Points.*

> *What had motivated the tremendous outpouring of hatred? On one level, the mob undoubtedly sought to emphasize its opposition to the abolition movement, and its implied message that blacks were the equal of whites. Yet the breath and*

---

[33] Dr. Tingba Apidta. *The Hidden History of New York*, The Reformation Project, 1998, p. 113

> *intensity of the attack against black Five Points indicate that members of the crowd, either consciously or unconsciously, harbored some deeper resentments.* Signs *of African American economic independence clearly galled them, for while the black-occupied hovels of a particularly decrepit alley known as "Cow Bay" were left untouched, the few black owned businesses in the neighborhood were devastated. Finally, by literally tearing the roofs off black-owned or occupied buildings, the mob sent perhaps its most emphatic and unmistakable message. The rioters sought to not merely injure black owned or occupied property, but to make their homes and businesses permanently uninhabitable.*[34]

The struggle for justice and equality for all that Vincente Guerrero began continues. I often wonder how he would relate to the modern Vincente Fox. One, a former illiterate slave who rose to be "the George Washington and Abraham Lincoln combined of Mexico," freed his country and then its slaves."[35] The other, is a former Coca-Cola executive and representative of a greedy corporate culture that appears to be gobbling up the whole world. The children of the European invaders of Mexico, whom Mr. Fox

---

[34] Tyler Anbinder, Five Points, 2001, The Free Press, p. 12
[35] Rogers, 1996, p. 182

represents, control vast tracks of land, resources and politicians there. The poor have no voice. Poor Mexicans risk life and limb to escape to America – where they believe more opportunities exist to make a living. Unfortunately, they are confronted with more racism when the reach the United States.

According to a 2004 report by the California based Tomas Rivera Policy Institute, the Latino population of North Carolina grew by 274 percent between 1990 and 2000. "The New Latino South and the Challenge to Public Education," said the Latino population in Gwinnett County, Georgia, which is outside Atlanta, has grown 657 percent, in the same period. The report found, however, that despite the large influx of Spanish speaking people used to fill low-skilled jobs, there has been no commitment, on the part of the municipalities benefiting from the labor, to educate non-English speaking children. That "lack of commitment is 'generating…de facto educational segregation in the South.'"[36]

Unfortunately, the immigration situation sets the stage for war between the poor masses that are in the U.S. and those entering the country to seek opportunities and advancement. The different groups often see each other as threats to the respective group's ability to survive. That is when the rich come back into the picture. They

---

[36] Miriam Jordan, *Report Warns Influx of Hispanics in South Creates School Crisis*, Wall Street Journal, 12.09.04

pit one against the other in order to continue exploiting poor people. At the height of the immigration debate, during the tenure of President Fox, he was insensitive enough to say Mexican migrants held jobs in the United States that "not even Blacks" want. Folks on both sides of the border were offended by the statement and offered different retorts and criticisms.

President Fox dismissed the criticisms and claimed his statement was misinterpreted. But weeks later, the government of Mexico issued a series of stamps that graphically depicted what his government thought of Black people.

[Memin Pinguin is a popular comic book character in Mexico. He is a black child, with thick white lips and wide-open eyes. "His appearance, speech and mannerisms are the subject of kidding by (w)hite characters in the comic book, which started in the 1940s and is still published in Mexico," wrote Mark Stevenson, for the Associated Press in June, 2005.]

Black people up north in the United States know about that kind of stereo-typing. Memin reminded me of a character racist White folks in the United States call Sambo. Hollywood, with few exceptions, has traditionally made Black people look sub-human.

From the infamous silent movie *Birth of a Nation*, at the beginning of the age of cinema, to the modern portrayals of Black urban low-lives in movies, music videos, television and stage, Black characters are limited to playing buffoons or inept regulation defenders of the status quo. Our women are portrayed as loose, and even our celebrated athletes and entertainers are described as naturally strong, rather than intelligent, like white people. The whole world has been fed these images for generations and even some Black folks have begun to believe the lies.

For more information on this and related subjects please consult: *The African Experience in Spanish America* (1936), by Leslie B. Rout; *The Chickasaw Freedmen* (1980), by Daniel Littlefield; *Forgotten Heroes* (1993), by Clinton Cox; *One Drop of Blood* (2000), by Scott L. Malcolmson; and *Bearing Arms for His Majesty* (2001), by Benjamin Vinsom III.

The previous examples can stand as microcosms for the life African and indigenous people have been forced to endure in the Americas for well over 500 years, as the next chapter will illustrate. Black people, who were the first to populate the Americas, as we will show, have been forced to live under an imposed Pigmentocracy that dates back long before Christopher Columbus was born. It has since morphed into the global rule of White and Yellow oligarchies. But the indigenous Black people of the earth have failed to realize from whence these other folks have come. We act as though

White and Yellow folks suddenly appeared on earth from outer space, as opposed to, from among ourselves in an ancient past.

(Photos on Previous Page:)
Children playing in Cuajiniquilapa, Mexico, 1998;
Children of Flower's Bank, Belize, 1999;
Lake Independence, Belize City, 1999;
Happy children in Lake Independence, Belize, 1999;

(This page)
Children running from tourists in Cape Coast, Ghana, 1996;
Children playing in Caribbean Sea inside the reef in Belize, Ambergris Caye, 1995.
All photos by Lamont Muhammad

Chapter Three
The Greatest Story Never Told

[Olmec stone head found at Tres Zapotes in southern Veracruz]

A: Early America

Neither the Mayas, not the Aztecs, Toltecs or other Native Americans built the first Pyramids in Mexico, although they built pyramids later on in the history of the region. Moreover, it is very likely that in parts of Mexico, particularly in the areas where the Olmecs resided, the Mexican Indian population may have been scarce or non-existent in that particular area, and may have arrived from the Northern parts of the Americas later on in history, as the Aztecs had. In fact, according to Frank C. Hibben, the Aztecs claimed that the pyramids were already in existence when they arrived in the Valley of Mexico, and these pyramids in Tenochitlan were built by the "Gods." In his book, Unexpected Faces in Precolumbian America, Alexander Von Wuthenau (1975) explained that American Indian types have not been found in the earliest human figurines unearthed at the major Olmec archeological sites, from the earliest times.

Modern Anthropologists have proven that the oldest remains of a human being in the western hemisphere is that of a Black women. She was found in Brazil in 1975 and named Luiza, after her namesake "Lucy," who was found in Ethiopia. Lucy was estimated to date back 3.2 million years; Luiza dates back 11,500 years. Luiza was unearthed in 1975, but was not officially recognized to be a Black woman until 1998, when archaeologists discovered her packed away. According to a Reuters piece that ran in *The Japanese Times*,

"Skull alters theory on colonization of Americas" (September 22, 1999), Archaeologist Walter Neves, who specializes in human paleontology, could not get over the big head impression on the fossil. The team finally realized that the head was that of an African woman.

[Belize Pyramid– Xunantunich, Belize, by Barry Tessman.]

According to historian Harold Sterling Gladwin (1883 – 1983), the first major waves of migration into the Americas were comprised of Black people from Asia. In his book, *Men Out of Asia* (1947), Mr. Gladwin reveals the documentation that shows the major migrations into the Americas consisted of Australoids (Aboriginals), Asiatic Negroids, Algonquins, and finally, Eskimos. He established the migrations of these diverse peoples by pinpointing their respective Old World cultural prototypes and technologies and by tracing and identifying them in their subsequent New World settings.[36]

Researcher Runoko Rashidi reviewed Gladwin's piece for *African Presence in Early America*, edited by Professor Ivan Van Sertima.

> *Gladwin's text is of particular importance to Afrocentric analyses of American history because it is one of the few substantial studies backed by specialized field research that claims that the earliest American populations were Black. It is our firm conviction, therefore, that in an age in which a completely new vision of the Black presence in world history is being espoused uncompromisingly, the "Gladwin Thesis" and the bold, compelling and factual manner in which it is presented, can not be ignored, overlooked or acknowledged.*
>
> *In spite of the forty years that have now elapsed since Men Out of Asia's initial publication, it will probably surprise few to know that the essential themes contained within it, or at least the portion*

---

[36] Ivan Van Sertima, 1992, Runoko Rashidi, *Men Out of Asia: A review and Update of the Gladwin Thesis*, p. 215-216

of it with which we are concerned, are still unknown to all but a comparatively small number of serious students, and remain unacceptable to Western academicians as a whole. When we add to this the fact that the text is now out of print and has not been available for some time, the necessity for a critical review and reassessment of the "Gladwin Thesis" from an Afrocentric perspective becomes all the more apparent.[37]

Gladwin theorized that the first major wave began 25,000 B.C. with a group of people he called "Australoids (derived from 'austral' or 'southern'), whom he described as relatives of the "Australian Aborigines." They referred to themselves as "Kooria ('Black people'). Similar Australoid descendant groups can be found today among the six-million Mundas of East and Central India, and the easily identifiable Veda populations of Sri Lanka."[38]

Gladwin called the second major wave "Asiatic Negroids," whom he described as Africans who entered the Americas from Asia, 15,000 years ago.[39] Rashidi preferred to call them "Clovis-Folsom Point Blacks," in his account, recognizing that second migration wave for the special hunting spear tips found in parts of ancient

---
[37] Ibid. p. 216.
[38] Ibid, p. 220
[39] Ibid, p. 223

South America, Central America, Mexico, the North American southwest, and Canada.

The third migration wave, the Algonquins, Gladwin said, arrived 1,000 B.C. Rashidi said subsequent carbon-14 dating methods pushed the dates back to 2,000 B.C. Archaeologists argue that this third wave represented the first non-African type to migrate into the Americas in large numbers.[40]

[Please note: The third wave of people to the Americas were known by their "cord-wrapped" or "Jomon pottery ware; the use of which was widely employed in Eastern Asia from about 11,000 to 300 B.C."[41] The evidence suggests the third wave was a second wave of Black people from China and India who found a refuge in the west from the bloodbath that was going on in the east. The third wave was also known for wearing the same Mohegan hairstyle the Olmec people were known for, according to Ego Hayes, a scholar whom we will discuss later.]

According to Gladwin's findings, the Eskimo was the fourth or final pre-Columbian major migration into the Americas, which occurred around 500 B.C.

> The arrival of the Eskimo along the Arctic Coasts marked a fundamental transition in the anthropological history of North America. It was the last of a series of long

---

[40] Ibid, p. 225
[41] Ibid, p. 226

> *headed migrations, and the broad faces and slant eyes of the Eskimo marked the initial stage of a long period of Mongoloid (Mongolian) domination in lands where Mongoloid people had therefore been unknown.*[42]

Olmec, is a name contemporary historians and archaeologists use to identify the art and culture produced by the people who set the stage for what is considered the first civilization in Mexico. Michael Coe, author of *Mexico,* said "(t)here is now not the slightest doubt that all later civilizations in Meso-America, whether Mexican or Maya, ultimately rest on an Olmec base." Professor Ivan Van Sertima of Rutgers University agreed. His work went further to show the "confluence(s)" that occurred between Africans and ancient America.

> *It is with Mexico, however, that we are most concerned, for here we can see the confluence of cultures, not just the confluence of bloods. When we compare the cult of the werewolf (the coyote of the prairies) found among the amanteca with the cult of the werewolf (the hyena of the savannahs) found among the Bambara of medieval Mali, we see quite clearly that we are at the very head of the confluence.*[43]

---
[42] Ibid, p. 226
[43] Ivan Van Sertima, *They Came Before Columbus*, Random House, 1976 p.94

[A footnote in Van Sertima's text described the Amanteca as a mixed trader/featherworker caste in medieval Tlateluco, the market island across the lake from Mexico-Tenochtitlan.]

Van Sertima showed that a Smithsonian/National Geographic Society team discovered colossal "Negroid heads" in Mexico in 1938.

> *Massive, military, menacing they stood, faces of pure basalt stone, dominating the vast ceremonial plaza in which they were found. The lines of cheek and jaw, the fullness of the lips, the broadly fleshed noses, the acutely observed and faithfully reproduced facial contour and particulars bore eloquent witness to a Negro-African presence. One of the Negroid colossi, eight and a half feet high and twenty-two feet in circumference, wore ear plugs with a cross carved in each. They wore headdresses that were foreign and distinctive – domed helmets like those of ancient soldiers. They all faced east, staring into the Atlantic.*[44]

Professor Edward Bynum of the University of Massachusetts agreed.

---

[44] *Ibid.*, p. 144-145

There are terra-cotta skulls of Africans found in great abundance among the Olmec... But more than this is in evidence and suggests a diffusion of certain elements of Kemetic (Egyptian) science, technology, and metaphysics throughout the Americas. As pointed out earlier, an Egyptian hieroglyphic-type script was found in use among the Micmac Indians (Fell, 1989; Maillard, 1921). The style is very similar to that in Egypt around 1400 B.C.E. Some (eighty percent) of the Wabanaki Indian vocabulary for astronomy is reportedly Egyptian. Further south in Mexico, both the stepped and conical pyramids suddenly appear in the Americas about the time of the dated Egyptian contact, but there is no prior history of their development in this region of the world. All at once they appear in full development! In Egypt and Nubia, it took centuries of experimentation to perfect the pyramid, and the earlier attempts are scattered across their landscape. The first such stepped pyramid appears in La Venta where large Negriod heads are found and when and where Olmec civilization first flourished. Another appears at Cholula, dedicated to Quetzalcoatl in 150 B.C.E., and another at Teotihuacan near Mexico City. The latter, like the Egyptian, has a movable capstone and is almost the exact size of the Great Pyramid of Egypt.[45]

Professors Van Sertima, Bynum, Dr. Charles Finch and others, are attacked for being Afro-centrists. They are accused of reinventing history by many of the traditional historians. A number attacked Van Sertima in the June 1997 edition of *Current Anthropology* with a piece entitled: "Robbing Native American Cultures."

> *To a lay observer, it seems at first glance that these gray, 'black' – looking heads, with thick lips and flat noses, must be images of Africans. This impression makes the other appear to be support for an obvious conclusion. However, this is a fundamental error. The people claimed by Van Sertima and other Afrocentrists to have influenced the Olmec (and to be models for the heads) are Nubians or Egyptians, that is North and East Africans, whereas the slave ancestors of African-Americans came primarily from tropical West Africa. The groups are very different and do not look alike. Flat noses are particularly inappropriate as racial markers, because the shape of the nose is primarily a function of climatic factors...*[46]

---

[45] Edward Bynum, *The African Unconscious,* Teachers College Press, Columbia University pgs. 60, 62
[46] Gabriel Haslip-Viera, Bernard Ortiz de Montellano, and Warren Barbour, *Current Anthropology Vol.38 #3, June 199, "Robbing Native American Cultures: Van Sertima's Afrocentricity and the Olmecs,"p.422*

Michael Coe, the Yale University archaeologist, contributed to the discussion in the comments section of the publication.

> *Van Sertima and his associates have committed the fallacy of taking a style of art as a racial fact. If this kind of reasoning were valid, then we should assume that all Hellenistic Greeks looked like Alexander the Great... The colossal heads really are portraits of Olmec rulers, but the physiognomies of those rulers were altered to fit the prevailing Olmec canons of monumental art. Olmec jade carvers had somewhat different canons, producing slightly 'Oriental' – looking figurines. Neither the great heads nor the figures are to be taken as phenotypical fact.*[47]

These are examples of modern day spin doctors who are intentionally or otherwise skewing important facts. Cheikh Anta Diop documented in his book, *The Cultural Unity of Black Africa*, that Egypt was a Black nation and that a thread ran and runs through Black Africa that binds all to a common root. What part of Africa these Black people with thick lips and broad noses came from is not the issue. The point is that Black people from a common African root exported what they knew to the west and did not come to pillage and subjugate, but to build and develop.

---

[47] Ibid., pgs. 432 – 433

The African contacts with the Olmec and other later Meso-American civilizations from what we can see were primarily through trade and cooperation. There was no invasion and colonization, no cataclysmic encounter or conflict, no conquistador tradition of Columbus, Cortez, Desoto, the Pizarro brothers (Francisco, Gonzalo, Juan and Hernando), no Pedro de Mendoza and thousands of others who brought death, disease, degradation, and slavery! The peoples involved in the early African contacts, in all likelihood, were from the kingdoms of Mali.

Mali at the time was a rich and powerful empire with contacts not only in the interior of Africa, but across Lake Chad to Egypt, Nubia, and Ethiopia, and also apparently across the seas to the Americas. This influence spread to Mexico and to a lesser extent the North American peoples. We have records and relics of these contacts in the cross-fertilization of technology, science and religion.[48]

Bynum fleshes out the African base of the Olmec civilization.

---

[48] Bynum, 1999, pages 63, 64

The Olmec kings, like the pharaohs, wore a duel crown, a symbol of Menes' great union of the North and South of Kemet (Egypt). Both had the royal flail; the plumed serpent suddenly replaces the royal jaguar; purple is the royal color. The Olmec books, most of which were burned deliberately by the Europeans, had black and red kingsin royal purple. Artificial beards appear on both, as they did on the African pharaohs. There is even the exact same royal pattern of three concentric circles and three colors to the feathered sunshade. There is the same loom style in Mexico and Peru as in Egypt. The complex lost wax technique, used in Egypt and ancient Nubia and then spread to West Africa's Yoruba and Bini peoples of Nigeria in the Medieval period after the collapse of Kemetic civilization, appears suddenly in the Americas with no gradual technological history (Van Sertima, 1976).

The Egypto-Nubian surgical technique of trephination, where a surgical hole is drilled in the skull to relieve pressure on the brain, is suddenly performed in both ancient Mexico and Peru by the hundreds in the identical fashion, with circular and square hole techniques. And the gods?

> *The Egypto-Nubian god Aton with no face and two ropes emerging from his mouth suddenly appears in Ancient Mexico.*[49]

B: <u>Out of Africa</u>

Ego Hayes, a retired N.Y.C. Public School Principal, former art major, and a student of world history, said all art, science and math started in Kemet/Egypt. Art majors, he explained, can read the symbols on the pyramids and other stone ruins that dot the ancient worlds. "Everything is art," the scholar argued.

"Writing is an art. Creating symbolism is art and it all began in Kemet (Egypt). Chinese calligraphy is the Medu Netr (Egyptian Sacred Writing), a picture writing from right to left, in vertical columns. When you study the symbols and structure of Arabic, Amharic, Hebrew, Sanskrit, and Chinese, you discover they all have a common root in Kemet," he explained to me during one of our sessions.

Professor James Small, of the Leonard Jeffries Harlem University (C.C.N.Y.) circle, introduced me to Bro. Ego. He described him as an expert on the African foundation of civilization in Mexico, China, and the rest of the world. He took me to Bro. Ego's home, where he was holding court on his front steps with his Harlem neighbors. We agreed to meet another day.

---

[49] Ibid., page 62

He and his regal wife, Cassianna were travelers. He taught me with the slides and photos they shot to illustrate and document that the glyphs in Mexico, Cambodia, Australia, and Egypt used the same symbols. An example is found in the fact that all of the said cultures revered the pygmy. The other symbols and signs on the sculptures and walls showed the art had one original source, the Kemetic Sacred Science of Egypt. Priests, he said, took the knowledge to other corners of the world in a Diaspora from Kemet/Egypt.

Bro. Ego also introduced challenged me to consider the Olmec civilization was brought to Mexico by survivors of the fall of the Shang Dynasty in China, in 1122 B.C. The same year is said to be the beginning of the Olmec civilization in Mexico. The colossal Olmec heads that are scattered around Mexico depict two types: African and Mongolian.

Did Africans escape an encroaching bloodbath in the east, and find a temporary refuge in the best part of the western hemisphere?

Contemporary civilization documents show they believed the earth was flat at a time when Black people were sailing the entire globe.

[Retired School Principle Ego Hayes at home in Harlem, 2002, by Lamont Muhammad]

C: <u>Out of China?</u>

Early Chinese legends relate traditions of divine dynasties, one being the Epoch of the Five Emperors. The first Emperor, known as Fu-His/Fu-hi (2953 B.C. – 2838 B.C.), is described as being a wooly-haired Negro. He is credited with establishing government, originating social institutions and cultural inventions. Similar to the Egyptian god Thoth, he "taught his people to fish with nets and rear domestic animals... [and] devised cultural inventions." Fu-his was the first to develop writing.[50]

The oldest human skeletal remains in China are those of Black or African people. Human beings living in China prior to 3200 B.C., are referred to as "primarily non-Chinese or Proto-Chinese," according to historian James Brunson. Proto means before or earliest, as in parent. African skeletal remains found south of the Yangtze River in China date back 8,000 years, he said.[51]

According to the Encyclopedia Britannica (U.C., 1968), the first three dynasties in China - the Hsia, Shang (Chiang), and Chou, grew out of the Lungshanoid (Black Pottery) culture.[53] The Hsia introduced writing and agriculture to China almost 5,000 years ago. The Shang Dynasty ruled China from 1766 B.C. to 1122 B.C. The Chou was a powerful clan that earned its stripes battling nomadic invaders (from Europe) on the western frontier.

---

[50] Ivan Van Sertima, *African Presence in Early Asia,* Transition Books (1992), *African Presence in Early China*, by James Brunson, p. 123.
[51] Ibid, p. 121
[52] University of Chicago, 1968, *Encyclopedia Britannica, China,* p.576

> *(They formed a coalition with) eight other states and gradually (20 years) overwhelmed the Shang and ruthlessly destroyed their capital in 1122 B.C. Blood flowed like a river at the battle. Survivors fled in every direction and may well have served as culture bearers to places as far removed as Hanan in the south and Manchuria and Korea in the north and northeast.[53]*

The Chou or Western Zhou ruled over many tribes in China for hundreds of years, after which, the Eastern Zhou, the last African-based dynasty in China ruled until 256 B.C. The end of Chou or Zhou rule closed out the Ancient era of China's long and bloody history.

The following Qin Dynasty (247 BC) started the Imperial era, which is famous for building the first of many Great Walls.

> *The Great Wall stretches over approximately 6,400 km (4,000 miles) from Shanhaiguan in the east to Lop Nur in the west, along an arc that roughly delineates the southern edge of Inner Mongolia, but stretches to over 6,700 km (4,160).[54]*

---

[53] Ibid, p. 576
[54] http://en.wikipedia.org/wiki/Great_Wall_of_China

The wall was built to keep Mongolians from invading China. Who were these Mongolians?

Dr. Cheikh Anta Diop called Mongolians a product of mixing, according to an essay by James Brunson.

> *The yellow race as well was probably the result of crossbreeding between Blacks and Whites at a very ancient time in history of mankind. In fact, the yellow peoples have the pigmentation of mixed breeds so much so that comparative biochemical analysis would be unable to reveal any great difference in the quality of melanin...and it has been observed that wherever there are yellow-skinned peoples, one still finds pockets of Black and Whites who seem to be residual elements of that race.*[55]

The Honorable Elijah Muhammad said the same thing in different terms.

> *This is the Chinese I am talking about. The China man is near equal with white folks. He loves to fight, but he's braver than whites, because he's back more closer to the father than the white.*[56]

The evidence suggests that Mongolians, a mixed people invaded the Black world before White folks did. The

---

[55] .Brunson, p. 120
[56] Elijah Muhammad, *Yacub: Father of Mankind*, Secretarius (2002) p. 87

record shows they started their invasions from the north in both hemispheres, but they got started in the east.

According to the history of the Great Wall, it was built along China's northern border with Mongolia. The following account, hundreds of years later, was from inside China.

> *The year is 550 B.C. China is at war. The violence is terrible. Some battles have up to 400,000 victims. (To put this in perspective, about 57,000 American soldiers died in the entire Viet Nam War.) They killed everybody – men, women, children, and old people. They did horrible things to the victims – like cutting them up and making them into soup. Then they made their relatives eat it...*[57]

D: <u>Out of Europe</u>

According to researcher, Paul L. Guthrie, author of *Making of the Whiteman*, the first record of trouble making on the planet began when White folks suddenly showed up in Europe around 6,000 years ago.

> *This change occurred in the area of the Caucasus Mountains. There, in West Asia, a previously unknown group of people suddenly appeared as if from out of*

---

[57] Tim Baker and Kate Etue, *Why So Many Gods?*, Thomas Nelson, Inc., 2002, p. 25

nowhere. Collectively they are known as the Indo-Europeans, Caucasians or white people. The facts show that they first entered the area around 6,000 years ago. (Two Thousand) years later their invasions would bring them into contact with the civilized nations of the south.[58]

The record shows these invasions began to hit Egypt approximately 4,000 years ago when Menes or King Narmer overthrew invaders from the north and reunited upper and lower Kemet/Egypt in 3,100 B.C. One of the ancient text, *The Admonitions of Ipu-Wer*, provided this account of White folks moving into Kemet.

Barbarians from outside have come to Egypt... the children of nobles are dashed against the walls... The storehouse is stripped bare; its keeper is stretched out on the ground... Behold now, something has been done which has never happened... he who never even slept on a plant is now the owner of a bed... Behold, the owners of robes are now in rags. But he who never wove for himself is now the owner of fine linen...

Behold, she who once looked at her face in the water is now the owner of a mirror.[59]

---

[58] Paul L. Guthrie, *Making of the Whiteman,* Beacon Communications (1992) p. 3
[59] Ibid, p. 9, 10

In addition, Rodolpho Benavides, Mexican born historian and author of the *Dramatic Prophecies of the Great Pyramid*, interpreted the sacred writings on the pyramid walls to agree that a new people came on the planet 6,000 years ago.

> *The Age of Adam began six thousand years ago, but it is well known that human beings existed on the planet many thousands of years before that time, though the precise number of thousands changes with each new anthropological discovery, pushing the appearance of true man farther and farther into the past. Adam's race, therefore, does not mean the first people on earth but refers to a dynamic ethnic group whose evolution has affected many other groups along a road that began theirs in common. Ultimately, the Age of Adam includes both gentiles and Jews, united in one destiny.[60]*

Dr. Rudolph Windsor, author of *From Babylon to Timbuctu*, reveals in his book a history of wars between "Germanic Nomads," or "Shepard Kings," and the original Black rulers of Egypt. Light skinned people came in as barbarians. After hundreds of years of wicked rule, or "the period of Great Humiliation," the Nubians in the south ran them back up into the north. Eventually, however, the barbarians returned, removed

---

[60] Rodolpho Benavides, Dramatic Prophesies of the Great Pyramid, Editores Mexicanos Unidos, 1974, p 363

the Black kings of Egypt, and set Black people on the run.

E: Out of Africa II

As late as the 1300s Black people were freely navigating the oceans, while barbarians, believing the earth to be flat, stayed in the east, where it all began. In an article for the June 1993 edition of the Arabic language *Mahjubah Magazine,* Laila Hasib wrote the story of King Abubakari II of Mali, who sailed west with 2,000 ships in 1311. His brother, Mansa Musa, was crowned king when Abubakari did not return from his second voyage. King Musa reported the events on his famous Hajj to Mecca in 1324, Ms. Hasib wrote.

Many modern scholars believe that the Garifuna people of Central and South America, are descendants of those seafaring African explorers. They still speak their own language and were never slaves, in fact, they successfully withstood invasions from French, Dutch, Portuguese, Spanish and British imperial forces for over 300-years. In 1796, the British finally forced the Garifuna to the table. When the negotiations were over, the British separated the group into Blacks and Browns and scattered them throughout the Central American region. Many Blacks were forced to settle on the island of Rotan, Honduras. There was little water there to sustain their numbers and many were forced to the Honduran mainland, convert to Catholicism and to accept Spanish names.

[Garifuna re-enact their arrival in Belize on November 19, 1823, seeking political asylum. (1999) by Lamont Muhammad]

It is interesting to note that the Garifuna were given coastal lands in the region because they plant and fish. Other cultures, including the indigenous, preferred to live in the highlands, for fear of hurricanes and flooding. Today, however, the increasing pressure of rich resort and marina developers are pushing the Garifuna off of the coasts. The drive for sun, sea and sand destinations, have forced them inland where many feel pressured to change their lifestyles.

[Members of the Garifuna community meet in Belize City. 1998. Photo credit: Lamont Muhammad]

Many in Belize, for example, are great organizers and educators. They remain a relatively tight community who not only cater to each other but to tourist, etc. They are credited with laying out the educational system in Belize because they are known to speak their language, Garifuna (which can be written with Arabic letters); Mopan Maya; Quiche Maya; Spanish and English.

They are also viewed as the community that has maintained their own traditional roots as Black Caribs who arrived in the Americas before others.

*Garinagu making "fu fu" in Dangriga, Belize, 1999.
Photo credit: Lamont Muhammad]*

F: <u>Out of Asia II</u>

Time ran out for the blessed Black people who found refuge in the Americas, when the same Mongolians China failed to keep out, discovered the Bering Strait.

Her Highness Verdiance Tiara Washitaw – Turner Goston El-Bey, was the first person to describe that missing link from American history. She was the first person I interviewed when I returned to the States with my pamphlet version of *Black Mexico* in 2000 [see *Appendix A*]. The Empress of the Muurs or Moundbuilders, reigns over the oldest indigenous nation in the Americas, according to a United Nations designation. She told me, during interviews in Louisiana in June, 2000, Mongolians entered the Americas through the Bering Strait, gathered their numbers in the northwest, and when they were strong enough, they ran us out. Those who remained were raped and robbed into the Hollywood version of the American Indian, the Empress said.

Later, I heard an author interviewed on radio who claimed Chinese explorers crossed the oceans and discovered America, some 70 years before Christopher Columbus was born. I quickly sent for a review copy of *1421: The Year China Discovered America* (*1421*), by Gavin Menzies. The publisher sent two by the time I got the first one. I gave one to Ego Hayes a few days before I was to attend the book launching at the New York Asia Society, in January, 2002.

The book argues:

- *The Chinese were the first to discover America...*
- *They reached Australia, 350 years before Cook*
- *They discovered Antarctica and the South Shetland Isles*
- *The fleets of Admiral Zheng He sailed through the Magellan Straits 60 years before Magellan was born*

- *They charted both the Atlantic and Pacific coasts of South America, bringing back artifacts. They established trade routes with Africa and India.*
- *They understood the concepts of longitude way before the Europeans*
- *The whole world was charted by 1428*
- *European explorers set sail armed with maps copied from the Chinese.*[61]

Ego Hayes, quite earnestly, described the book, as the latest in a long series of would be new revelations that were designed to confuse the efforts of scholars like Van Sertima. He told me most of what Mr. Menzies attributed to the Mongolian Chinese in his book, had already been accomplished by the Olmecs or Africans nearly 2,000 years earlier.

[61] From a press release entitled *The Year China Discovered America*, by Gavin Menzies

[(At left) Brother Candy is picking coconuts. (At right) On Ambergris Caye, Belize, 1997. Photo credit: Lamont Muhammad.]

[Please note, however, the Chinese features of Bro. Candi. He told me his mother is Maya and his father is Garifuna. The Yellow Chinese did show up on the regional shores at some point.]

Menzie's multimedia presentation included large graphics which he used to transport the packed house around the world with the aide of a laser-pointer.

But Menzie's version of history is just another attempt to hide the facts of history, according to scholars like Mr. Hayes. The gatekeepers would rather attribute to Mongolians, what was accomplished by Black people thousands of years earlier. They do not want to suggest that survivors of the Shang Dynasty escaped China, and helped to establish the Olmec civilization in Mexico, Ego said, in words.

After the brilliant presentation, a friend persuaded me to quiz Menzie in the autograph line. When I finally reached the end of the very long line, the retired Royal British Submarine-commander admitted to me that the historical view presented by Bro. Ego was "reputable."

****

The critics received *1421* with praise and scorn, for a variety of reasons. P.B.S. (Public Broadcast television) dedicated an entire show to the debate. One Chinese expert argued that some of what Menzies attributed to his people in *1421* would have been impossible. He said there are no recordings of longitude and latitude calculations in the Chinese archives until centuries later. In fact, he said, the records of that time show the Chinese believed the world was flat.

In another piece the Asia Society handed out titled *2,500 Years Before Columbus*, evidence is provided to suggest a Chinese origin of Olmec civilization, but Africans were not mentioned.

> *It turns out that when the last Shang King was defeated and killed by rivals in 1122 B.C., his loyalists were forced to flee to*

> the "East Ocean" or Pacific, notes Xu in his new book, Origin of the Olmec Civilization (University of Central Oklahoma Press, 1996). "Olmec civilization suddenly emerged around or immediately after the Shang's fall," he writes. "Was it just coincidence? Or is it possible that part of those 25,000 refugees from ancient China ended up in the New World/"

Another piece the Asia Society passed out: *Olmec Writing*, was more informative.

> *An Olmec origin for many pre-Classic Maya, would explain the cover-up of the jaguar stucco mask pyramids with classic Maya pyramids at these sites. It would also explain Schele and Freidel's (1990, p. 56) claim that the first king of Palengue was the Olmec leader U-Kix-chan; and that the ancient Maya adopted many Olmec social institutions and Olmec symbolic imagery...*

The piece said the Olmec language was an aspect of the Mending languages spoken in West Africa.

> *The Mande people often refer to themselves as Sye or Si 'black, race, family, etc.' The Si people appear to have been mentioned by the Maya. A.M. Tozzer*

> (ed.), *Relacion de las Casa de Yucatec Maya* said that the Tutul Xiu (shiu), a group of foreigners from zuiva, in Nonoualoco territory taught the Maya how to read and write. This term Xiu agrees with the name Si, for the Manding people (also it should be noted that in the Manding languages the plural number is formed by the suffix-u, -wu.
>
> The Olmec script is a logosyllabic script. The Olmec had both a syllabic and hieroglyphic script. The hieroglyphic signs were simply Olmec syllabic signs used to make pictures.[62]

I would argue that Gladwin's fourth migration into the Americas was Mongolian mountain people who discovered, through the Bering Strait, that the earth was round. I believe the people looked just like the Yellow people who had already slaughtered Black people into near extinction in China. I believe they settled in the northwestern corner of North America until their numbers grew numerous enough to move down and across to drive Black folks further into the bush, as the Empress explained. By the time the White folks discovered the earth was round, thousands of years later, we had been slaughtered and raped.

---
[62] Clyde Winters, from the Olmec Writing piece handed out at Menzie's book signing

G: **Out of Europe II**

The fifth major wave of migration into the Americas, of course, was made up of White people. Ironically, they were guided by Blacks, according to historical records. When White folks "discovered" America, it was already comprised of settlements. The Mongolians/Chinese, for the most part, had already destabilized black settlements and sent survivors running. That explains, for me, why the Europeans had help when they arrived on the shores of Mexico. Little did their helpers know that they would later become victims of those whom they helped.

> *As Cortes moved toward the Mexican capital with his gang of four hundred Spaniards, supported by thousands of native tribesmen happy to rebel against what they considered Montezuma's tyrannical rule, more messengers reached Tenochtitlan describing the newcomers as supernatural creatures riding on hornless deer, proceeded by wild animals on leashes, dressed in iron, armed in iron, fearless as gods.*
>
> *Spaniards say that when Cortes reached the city of Cholula, with its hundreds of whitewashed temples over which loomed the remnants of the largest pyramid in the*

Americas, his ambassador, whom he had sent ahead to seek peaceful surrender of the city, was returned with severed wrists dangling from flayed elbows. True or not, Cortes massacred six thousand Cholulans.[63]

The first murderer was getting a taste of a new murderer. The meek had already been set to flight. Many of the Africans who had traditionally traded and settled with the indigenous for centuries, were under attack, according to Spanish accounts.

Ferdinand Columbus, one of the four sons of Columbus, said "my father told me he saw Negroes north of Honduras." Then there is Vasco Nunez de Balboa coming down the slopes of Quarequa, which is near Darien, which we now call Panama. We have it down to the day – 25 September 1513. He sees two tall Black men among the native Americans. This is not the era of the African slave trade. The Spanish were utterly startled (so startled that four of them comment on it) and they asked the natives from whence did these Black men come. They did not know. All that they knew was that they lived in a large settlement nearby and they were waging

---
[63] Clyde Winters, from the *Olmec Writing* piece handed out at Menzie's Book signing

war with them and had captured two. These Africans are described in detail. Exceedingly black, a foot-and-a-half taller than the average Native American, of military bearing. Peter Martyr, the first historian of the European contact period, said that these Blacks must have been shipwrecked long ago from Africa (he called it Ethiopia which was then a general word for Africa from the word aethiops, meaning burnt skin). You also have other commentators like Lopez de Gomara who wrote that "these blacks Balboa saw were identical with the blacks we have seen in Guinea". Rodrigo de Colmenares reported that one of the captains of Balboa saw blacks east of the Gulf of San Miquel".

Then Alphonse de Quatrefages, author of "The Human Species" presents us with a map drawn by a French sea-captain, Kerhallet, showing independent black settlements in the area later called Brazil. Also, at the tip of Florida, and on the island of St. Vincent. This can account for the Charruas of Brazil, the Jamassi of Florida, and the Black Caribs of St. Vincent. They were all pre-Columbian Black settlements. Captain Kerhallet *presents a map of these settlements and that is the area, that very area, that is the endpoint or terminus of currents flowing in across the Atlantic from Africa. The Africans appeared exactly where the ocean current from Africa takes you.*[64]

Columbus also documented in his journal that the natives told him the gold-tipped spears they presented him with were gifts from tall Black men from the south. The record shows that he sent the spears back to Spain, "where metallurgists of Ferdinand and Isabella's land, newly liberated from the African Moors, found that they were identical in composition to those from Guinea and further south in Africa."[65]

****

Black people have much history to retrieve from the editorial cuts that have been left off of the pages of modern records. According to Ego Hayes, the White people who control the printing of history are never interested in truth that promotes other people at their own expense (see *Appendix G*). During one session he showed me footage of himself and Alexander Von Wuthenau, author of *Unexpected Faces In Ancient America*, taken at the author's Mexico City home. The

---

[64] Ivan Van Sertima, *Early America Revisited,* Transaction Publishers, 1998, p. 150 –151.
[65] Bynum, (1999), p 58,59.

German anthropologist was first introduced to most Black researchers by Professor Van Sertima. He has collected a number of Olmec and other ancient artifacts over a period of 50 years in Mexico, he explained to Van Sertima. He plainly stated in his book that Africans brought the light of civilization to the Americas. Mr. Von Wuthenau told his guests that day, Bro. Ego recalled to me during an interview, that he was warned against waking up the world to the African origins of Mexican civilization.

"White folks warned Von Wuthenau at a major New York City museum years ago that if he ever said Africans came to the Americas first he'd never work again," he told me.

Not much has changed in New York. A good example is found in new blockbuster movie by Oliver Stone, "World Trade Center." The movie centers on the heroic efforts of two former U.S. Marines who did not run from the burning World Trade Towers in New York, on "9-11." In fact, they volunteered to help find and rescue Port of Authority officers from beneath 20 feet of twisted metal, broken concrete and other hazardous debris at the site. One of the heroes was a Black man simply known as Sgt. Thomas. But in the film, actor Tom Cruise's white cousin played the role of Jason Thomas, according to a piece in the *Pittsburgh Post Gazette*, by L.A. Johnson, August 16, 2006.

H: **Are Black People Victims of Revenge?**

On January 2, 1492, "the African leader Abu Abdi-Llah, otherwise known as Boabdil, surrendered to the Spanish."[66] The event bought to an end a near 800-year rule of the Iberian Peninsula by the Moors.

> *The Moors transformed the Iberian Peninsula... They not only brought advanced drainage and irrigation systems, reservoirs, aqueducts, sophisticated storage facilities and efficient marketing, transportation and trading networks but they brought the beauty and freshness of the countryside into the cities – fantastic gardens, parks, lush inner courtyards and a constant supply of clean water.*[67]

The Moors introduced cotton, rice, sugar cane, dates, lemons and strawberries to Spain (John G. Jackson's *Introduction to African Civilization, 1970*). Van Sertima added coffee, syrup, soda and alcohol to the list.[68] Africans were responsible for introducing many of the instruments that spread from Spain to the rest of Europe, including the lute (predecessor to the guitar), the Pastoral flute, the Moorish pipes, two kinds of flagalet, and bagpipes. The percussion instruments

---
[66] Ivan Van Sertima, *Golden Age of the Moor*, Transaction Publishers, 1992, p. 13
[67] Ibid., p. 14
[68] Ibid., p. 11

include the bambrel, tambourines, castanets, brass rattles, macara, and atambor, according to an essay, "The Music of Spain, by Yusef Ali." [69]

Interestingly, Professor Ivan Van Sertima argues in his essay, *The Moor in Africa and Europe*, that Africans had, in fact, invaded Spain and established a presence in Europe a thousand years before Christ.

> *It is generally assumed that the movement of Africans into Europe, in significantly large numbers and into positions of power, did not occur until the Muslim invasion of Spain in 711 A.D. In Al-Makkary's History of the Mohammedan Dynasties in Spain, however, we learn of a great drought that afflicted Spain about three thousand years, a catastrophe that was followed not long afterwards by an invasion from Africa. This, of course, had nothing to do with the medieval Moors, with which this book is primarily concerned, but is worth noting here because it actually established an ancient African dynasty in Spain, a fact that is omitted from the official histories.* [70]

Many historians have described the Moorish occupation of Spain as an imposition of grand culture and civilization, in the place of underdevelopment, illiteracy and savagery. Slavery, however, played a central role

---
[69] Ibid., p. 316
[70] Ibid., p. 1

in the occupation. In fact, before the Europeans initiated the Trans-Atlantic slave trade, Africans were selling Europeans, but, under the Africans, European "(s)laves had rights and they could actually seek assistance if they were exceedingly maltreated."[71] In addition, the Moors encouraged education in Spain.

> *At a time when the most insignificant provinces of Moorish Spain contained libraries running intothousands of volumes, the cathedrals, monasteries and palaces of Leon, under Christian rule, numbered books only by the dozen. The paltry number of texts the Christians did possess were almost all devotional or liturgical.*[72]

Nevertheless, in 1492, enemies of the Moorish occupation of Spain were able to use the gunpowder the Moors manufactured in Spain, to drive the Moors out. The victory opened the door for Spain to roam the seas. It is widely believed that Christopher Columbus stumbled into the Americas looking for a western route to India. According to Horace Butler, author of *When Rocks Cry* Out, Columbus knew exactly where he was going when he "discovered" the Americas, and the refuge Black people had once enjoyed in the Americas up until the discovery of the Americas was made by the Mongolian people earlier.

---

[71]Ibid., p. 12
[72]Ibid., p. 13

> *It was the presence of ancient Egypt's Jerusalem, in the Americas, that kept scholars quiet, and preachers fearful, when I showed them the old maps and the ancient writings...and the forbidden histories.*
>
> *There were others who knew the forbidden histories. Even Christopher Columbus knew these secrets. He wrote that South America's Orinoco River flowed out of "Paradise," where Adam and Eve had lived. I was stunned to see that Columbus had promised he would recapture Jerusalem when he reached the Americas.*[73]

For the Spanish, however, they discovered a people in the west who looked like those whom they had just shaken off in the east. It also represented a new era of burning books and rewriting history. Cardinal Ximenes de Cisneros, of Spain, ordered African and Arab libraries burned, which "inspired a similar bonfire of the books of native Americans. Diego de Landa, the first Bishop of the Yucatan, exhorted his followers in 1562 to 'burn them all – they are works of the devil.'"[74]

According to Van Sertima, the book burnings had more to do with bigotry than religion.

---

[73] Horace Butler, *When Rocks Cry Out*, Stone River Publishing, 2009, p. 17
[74] Van Sertima, 1992., p. 13

> *Hatred of the dark invaders kindled the bonfires. The Church at that time too saw most of this foreign learning as something evil, even demonic. The number system that we use today, for example, brought in by the Moors from India, was seen as late as the 17th century in some parts of Europe as signs of the devil. It became a religious mission for men like Ximenes and his successors to erase from history all memory of the Moors. Ximenes even induced the Spanish sovereigns to outlaw public baths, making cleanliness antithetical to godliness.*[75]

By the time the Spanish encountered the Maya, however, there were new people sitting on the throne in Mexico.

> *We know that non-Maya or "Mexicanized Maya people from Tabasco and Central Mexico invaded, and that these new peoples flourished for a while in great urban centers like Chichen Itza. But by the time the Spanish conquered most of the Maya lands in the 1540s hardly a trace of the once great civilization with its profound and ancient spirituality was left.*

---

[75] Ibid., p. 13

What the Maya themselves had not destroyed of their own occult wisdom the Spanish finished off. Diego de Landa, the first bishop of the Yucatan, collected the remaining Maya books and burned them in a huge public bonfire. He also enforced Church laws so severely that he was recalled to Spain in 1568 by the Inquisition for his harsh treatment of his Maya charges. The Spanish conquistadors rounded up the Maya from the lowland cities and drove them on forced marches into the mountains to the south. Those who remained became the slaves of the conquerors. With the burning of the books and the destruction of the last Maya cities, what was left of the Maya secret wisdom was lost.[76]

Following murder and mayhem in Mexico and judgment in Spain, de Landa returned to Yucatan to write the "true Rosetta Stone for the deciphering of Maya hieroglyphic writing." Archaeologists continue to use de Landa's key to translating Maya sacred writings.[77]

It is important to note here, that modern archaeologist agree the Maya and Aztec civilizations sat on an

---

[76] Douglas Gillette, M.A., M. Div., *The Shaman's Secret,* A Bantom Book, 1997, p.13
[77] Michael D. Coe, *Breaking the Maya Code*, 1992, page 100

Olmec base. That means a Black, or Egyptian base, as quiet as it is kept.

Is it merely a coincidence that Black people are found in Mexico today, where the Olmec civilization was yesterday? Black Mexicans are found in Veracruz, on the southeast coast, and in the Costa Chica. The evidence suggests that the Veracruz region was headquarters for the Olmec civilization and mission outposts have been discovered in the Costa Chica.

Many attribute the large number of Black people in Mexico's southwest to the fact that the largest silver mine in the Western Hemisphere is there. According to historian, Dr. Leonard Jeffries, hundreds of thousands of Africans were brought there in chains by "converted Jews during the colonial era to die in the silver mines."

The researcher must recall the fact that Professor Beltran (*Chapter Two*) argued that there were 250,000 Black people living in that region before the Spanish, or the contemporary slave trade arrived.

The evidence suggests that Black people were the first to enjoy the abundant earth. Suddenly Black people were driven from the centers of power in the east by other than Black people who believed the earth was flat. The invaders in the east had no concept of more land across the oceans in the west. They were masters of death and destruction. Survivors of the onslaught against the original Black owners of the earth in the east, found a temporary refuge from the hatred and murder in the west.

But eventually, the secret about the preserved lands in the west was revealed to the barbarians in the east. Then the hatred and murder that was born in the east was visited upon what would eventually be named the Americas.

According to Horace Butler, author of *When Rocks Cry Out*, the wars in the west against Black people were initiated by Blacks against Blacks, or Africans against Africans. This idea will be further explored in the *Epilogue*. Nevertheless, based on history, these wars began with Blacks on Blacks to Yellow on Blacks to Whites on Blacks and Yellow.

Photo above: Miamisburg Mound, Ohio (online)

Author in Giza, Egypt, 1994 by James Muhammad

Monks Mound (on-line);

Black Mexico: The Greatest Story Never Told

*Author's son at Step Pyramid at Lamanai, Belize, 1995.
Photo credit: Lamont Muhammad*

Sakkara Pyramid, Courtesy of the Egyptian Tourism Board

Black Mexico: The Greatest Story Never Told

Chapter Four

THE HOUSE OF GOD

[Artist Nelson Young standing before his painting Redemption, Caye Caulker, 2002. Photo credit: Lamont Muhammad]

For the time is come that the judgment must begin at the house of God; and if it first begins at us, what shall the end be of them that obey not the gospel of God?[78]

---

[78] Scofield, C.I. (1967). *The New Scofield Reference Bible.* New York: Oxford University Press. p. 1336

Modern scholars agree that Arabic, Hebrew, Aramaic and other Semitic languages can be described as corrupted versions of a language that was spoken by Ancient Africans.

> *How is it that almost all the wandering tribes of Africa have always spoken Arabic, the language of Moses and of Job?"*[79]

Two scholars make the point with the following prayer.

Asr, Time Through the Ages

*In the Name of Allah, Most Gracious,
Most Merciful
By the token of Time (through the ages)
Verily Man Is in loss Except such as have Faith,
And do righteous deeds,
And join together
In mutual teaching of Truth,
and of Patience and Constancy*[80]

Muslims say the above prayer daily, between noon and sunset.

Is it a coincidence, before Moses, Jesus, and Muhammad, according to the Egyptian Book of the

---

[79] Rafiq Bilal and Thomas Goodwin. (1985). *Egyptian Sacred Science in Islam*. San Fransico: Bennu Publishers. p. 24
[80] Yusef Ali, *Holy Qur'an*, Sura 103

Dead, that Ra, the Sun God, went to the Ante Chamber two hours before sunset – daily – to transform himself into Asar, the Resurrection God?

No! The two names are from the same Ancient Arabic root.[81]

Those who prayed to Asar, the Resurrection God, had to maintain faith in His eventual victory, even in the apparent victory of Set or Satan.[82]

Are there signs in Mexico that address resurrection?

"When the sun sets on the (pre-Aztec) pyramid at Teotihuacan (Where the gods are born) in Mexico, it is rising on the Egyptian Sphinx, posed in an attitude of expectancy," a caption for an illustration reads in Rodolpho Benavides' *Dramatic Prophecies of the Great Pyramid*.[83] The book suggests that Mexico could very well be the incubator from which the rebirth of humanity will take place. He describes the Great Pyramid in Egypt as a book that outlines a 6,000-year rebellion or "Age of Adam" in a chronological history written in advance, based on his interpretations of the pyramidal inch markings. The walls of the passageways and rooms of the Great Pyramid tell a story that plays out over a period of exactly six

---

[81] Bilal and Goodman, p. 24
[82] Ibid., p. 32
[83] Benavides, Rodolpho. (1974). *Dramatic Prophesies of the Great Pyramid*, Editores Mexicanos Unidos. p. 71

thousand and one years: from 4000 B.C. to 2001 A.D. [84] In the Judgment chamber "The Great Judge of Nations," is seated on a thrown looking across the Atlantic Ocean at America. His call awakens, or resurrects a dead people in the west, back to a more elevated level then they had ever experienced before their fall. The establishment of the Kingdom of God follows the drama, Benavides explained.

> *The last chapter of the Egyptian Book of the Dead tells us that Osiris, the god of death and resurrection, moves in the opposite direction of the sun, from west to east. This may signify a rebirth for mankind, with its origins in the west.* [85]

That sounds like the teachings of the Honorable Elijah Muhammad, to me. He taught his followers that the "Original People" of the earth, the ancient people of the Sun - most of whom are on the bottom of the world they built - are the same ones whom God would visit and choose at the end of this age of might over right. Black folks, especially in the west, faced persecution, lost and prosecution. The process has cleansed the rejected and despised into new people, he said, three quarters of a century ago.

In the *ABCs of Islam*, published in the early 1970s, by New York's Temple No. 7, a young and Honorable Louis Farrakhan described Black people,

---
[84] Ibid., p. 202.
[85] Ibid., p. 306

including the Indians, as the Jesus on the cross. He said our hands are nailed – we cannot work for self. Our feet are nailed – we cannot roam free on the earth, our home. Around our head is a crown of thorns – false education and religion. And we bleed for the world, from our side, at the bottom of civilization, the Minister said.

****

> *White people go to church and speak about God. We dance in the temple and become God.*[86]

What becomes apparent when one researches culture and religion is that the more ancient the culture, the closer they saw themselves to a divine plan. The Maya, for example, apparently believed human beings have a divine potential.

> *The understanding that gradually dawned on me, the puzzle that was filling in and taking shape before my eyes, was that the Maya shamans had encoded in their art and writings a system for transforming the human soul into a durable being capable of defeating death and embracing immortality – a kind of 'resurrection technology.' This technology included achieving altered states of consciousness*

---

[86] Davis, Wade. (1999). *Shadows in the Sun.* New York: Broadway Books

> sacred objects, ritual practices, and in which oneness with the Divine Being was possible... I was discovering something within myself – an iridescent core – and a more vivid, passionate, and courageous way of living.[87]

Contemporary cultures borrow what they want from the original revelations.

> Gospel episodes appear to have actually been lifted from the Egyptian originals and given a Palestinian dressing. In the Temple of Luxor, built in 1700 B.C., there are four scenes in a vignette which show the Annunciation, the Conception, the Birth, and Adoration of the Child, here depicted as Horus, in later Christian iconography as Jesus.[88]

Christianity borrowed from the original African source, but weakened it. They have apparently left out the responsibility each individual has in their own salvation. The ancient Egyptians believed the human body is a prison house of the soul but through the disciplines of Arts and Sciences, the soul can be freed and advanced from the "level of mortal to that of God."[89]

---

[87] Gillette, Douglas. (1997). *The Shaman's Secret: The Lost Resurrection Teachings of the Ancient Maya*. New York: A Bantam Book. p. xii
[88] Finch, Charles. (1989) *Egypt Revisited, The Works of Gerald Massey: Studies in Kamite Origins*. Van Sertima. New Brunswick: Transaction Publishers. p. 410
[89] James, George G.M. (1954).*Stolen Legacy*. New York: Philosophical Library. p. 1

Dr. Charles Finch III, at the Medical School at Morehouse College, said the Mummy, or the Karast, whom the Greeks called Christos and the Christians call Christ, is not a Pharaoh set to resurrect at the end of time, but the sign of a body of people who would make a spiritual ascent back into the Father, God, or the First Good King. Dr. Finch describes himself as a great admirer of Gerald Massey, a self-taught British poet, journalist and Cryptologist. Mr. Massey's contribution to this discussion comes with his interpretation of *The Egyptian Book of the Dead*.

Dr. Charles S. Finch III lectures on the Dogon in Harlem. (by Lamont Muhammad)

There is nothing in all poetry considered as the flower of human reality more pathetic than the figure of Horus in Sekhem. He has grappled with the Apap of evil and wrestled with Sut – the devil or Satan – and been overthrown in the

> *passage of absolute darkness. Blind and bleeding from many wounds, he continues to fight with death itself; he conquers, rises from the grave like a warrior with one arm. Not that he has lost an arm; he has only got one arm free from the bonds of death, the bandages of the mummy made for the burial. But he lives, he rises again triumphant, lifting the sign of the Dominator aloft; and in the next stage of transformation he will be altogether freed from the trammels of the mummy to become pure spirit, in the likeness of the father as the express image of his person...* [90]

Wade Davis, author of *Shadows in the Sun,* defined "the Vodoun pantheon" in similar terms.

> *To Haitians this reclamation of the dead is not an isolated sentimental act; on the contrary, it is as fundamental and inescapable as birth itself. One emerges from the womb an animal, the spiritual birth at initiation makes one human, but it is the final reemergence that marks one's birth as sacred essence.* [91]

---

[90] Massey, Gerald. (1973). *Ancient Egypt, Light of the World.* New York: Samuel Weiser. p.87
[91] Davis 1998, p. 62

Epilogue

The Life of This World

The life of this world is simply like water. We send it down from the clouds so that the produce of the earth, where of people and cattle eat, grows with this (water) abundantly until when the earth (by means of it) receives its excellent ornature and has decked itself fairly beautiful and its owners feel sure that they are its masters, unexpectedly We command its destruction either by night or by day, so We render it a field that is mown down as though nothing had existed there the day before. Thus do We explain in detail the signs for a people who reflect.

Holy Qur'an 10:24 (Noorruddin)

If there is a major take away this writer wants to impress on readers of this project, it is that the majority of human beings in the world are victims of a global conspiracy to hide the fact that Black people were the first to settle and develop Asia (Earth) and the Americas, especially. Most human beings believe that Black people are worthless, and a hinderance that were brought to the Western Hemisphere in chains by White people to build this country for them, for free.

The truth is that Black people both enjoyed the West as a refuge from much of the violence that continues to plague the East, and some of us were exiled to the Americas for practicing polytheism some 16,000 years ago. Unfortunately, as this project will illustrate, many thousands of years before the exile, Black people from Africa did come across the Atlantic to make war with the Africans who had built the first Kemet (Egypt) in the Americas from Mexico to Brazil, including, as Horace Butler's research shows, other parts of the Americas. The new Africans, as he wrote, drove the descendants of original Africans who did build civilization here, back to modern Egypt, up the muddy Jordan to build replicas of the first Ancient Kemet (Egypt) there, wrote Horace Butler, author of *When Rocks Cry Out*.[92]

(Note: Egypt is a Greek word for Kemet. The name Egypt never existed during ancient times. It was invented to both steal the real name from history books and to remove the vibratory power of the name Kemet, said Mfundishi Jhutyms Ka N Heru El-Salim, author of *Spiritual Warriors are Healers*.)

In his book, Mr. Butler wrote about the relationship between the Americas and Ancient Kemet:
It was the unmistakable presence of Egypt's Great Pyramids at Teotihuacan, Mexico that unlocked the

---

[92] Butler, Horace. (2009). *When Rocks Cry Out*. Texas: Stone River Publishing. P. 76, 77.

"Forbidden Histories" and the secret locations of Egypt's cities in the Americas...When I shared with the scholars that the pyramids at Teotihuacan were the famed Great Pyramids, they took me for a fool and slowly pointed out to me – always with a smile – that my work must be a simple error of a simple mind, because the Great Pyramids could very easily be seen standing along the Nile in northeast Africa. I took no great joy in their misery when I pulled out a small green book and pointed to this single ancient description of one of the Great Pyramids:

"This pyramid was made like a stairway with tiers, or steps."

That simple description, alone, destroyed the scholars' argument that the pyramids in northeast Africa were the Great Pyramids called Wonders of the World. That description of the Great Pyramids as enormous, stepped pyramids came from Herodotus, who had seen the Great Pyramids. He described them being built in a tiered design, and the two Great Pyramids at Teotihuacan showed that tier design. The two great pyramids in Africa are smooth-sided and have no tiers!

In fact, Butler wrote that the original Africans built cities north of Mexico (Lower Egypt) and as far south as Peru (Upper Egypt), which he described (Peru) as a shortened version of Per Heru, the first Jerusalem.

His research included a conversation he had had with a Latina librarian who worked "in the Special Collections Library of a local university." [93]

> She knew the records that preserved Spain's early descriptions of the Americas. After being introduced to her, I went straight to the riddle that had consumed me. "I'm looking for the black people called Kali who were in the Americas when the conquistadors arrived."
>
> The slight smile fell from the librarian's mouth. She glanced around the dimly lit room, apparently to determine if anyone overheard my question. She walked me quickly to a table away from the ears of the few people near the entrance.
>
> "I can tell you where to find the Blacks who were in the Americas when Columbus came here," she whispered, as she leaned toward me for confidentiality. "But, you do understand that people do not like to talk about that, don't you?"[94]

---

[93] Ibid, p. 28
[94] Ibid, p. 28, 29

She went on, he wrote, to describe the fact that "the Caribs, the Black Caribs,"[95] were in the Americas before Columbus arrived, the same people we discussed earlier as the Garifuna (*Chapter Three/E*).

Mr. Butler opened my mind to a hidden world of answers I had been looking for with his research. For one, he explained the lingering hatred and frustration that Black people have demonstrated against one another, long before the arrival of White people and their form of civilization, an oppositional imitation of the original. Although some of the book's conclusions conflict with mine, the differences are minor, compared with the similarities. For example, he showed that the Spanish were determined to hide the fact that Africans were in the Americas before Columbus.

> *From the time the Spanish arrived in Mexico, official efforts to erase the African presence was pursued with a vengeance.*[96]

The book also helped me to see, as the quote from the Holy Qur'an (10:24) suggests, that "Africans" began to believe that they owned the planet, as opposed to The Originator of Creation who desires equality for all, not the idea of ownership and the desire by some to feel themselves superior to others. The idea set us up for a global purging that we continue to

---
[96] Ibid p. 42

experience, I believe. Many scholars disagree with Butler's premise but it helps me to see that Almighty God, Allah, is not a racist, and that He has a plan to bring us together.

My Research

Over the near 17 years I have worked on *Black Mexico*, the reoccurring theme on my mind is best expressed in a title of a book by Dr. Edward Bynum of the University of Massachusetts. *The African Unconscious: Roots of Ancient Mysticism and Modern Psychology*, actually tells the story this project was designed to argue. The book takes readers around the world to show all modern cultures sit on an African foundation. Other scholars support Dr. Bynum's argument by documenting the fact that the oldest fossil remains ever discovered in the Americas, China, and Africa (see *Chapter three*) are of Black people. In the Americas, for example, Luiza, as archaeologists have named her, was unearthed in Brazil and is estimated to have lived there more than 11,000 years before the trans-Atlantic slave trade was initiated. She undoubtedly had a mother and father.

That part of the story is clear to me and is probably deeply encoded in my D.N.A., like the people I met in Cuajinicuilapa. But again, people want to know how and why the first people are on the Bottom of the modern world?

Did God command, through Yellow and White nations, that Black nations be "mown down" as if civilized Black people never existed before?

Despite my recognition of the brilliant insights, research and study of the historians, scholars and other experts I have cited in this project, I believe most were intellectually confined to 6,000 years of history. Unfortunately, they were relegated to reading history in the language and schools of their/our open enemies, as THEM described them. Western Civilization begins with Menes marching an army north to reclaim Lower Kemet (Northern Egypt). History records that he reconnected Upper Kemet (Southern Egypt) with Lower Kemet (Northern Egypt) in or around to 3100 B.C. Modern Anthropologist and Archeologists refer to earlier periods as "pre-history" (to be fleshed out later in this chapter).

THEM's teaching is often viewed as a form of religion. Muslims who follow his teaching are called "Black Muslims." A Muslim, however, is one who submits his or her will to do the will of Almighty God, Allah, which sounds like religion. But as his Followers and the Holy Qur'an states, Islam is actually a way of life that was revealed "as a religion."

In that sense and as the purpose of this project, THEM's teaching of world history is offered as an alternative to the world history that we have been given. It is meant to make the reader think outside of a box. The gift makes viewing world history through a 6,000 year lens like judging life from one sentence in a large book that was taken from a hidden - infinite number of volumes. If Mr. Butler's argument is to be believed, whether knowingly or unknowingly, most said writers and scholars have an agenda to hide the evidence of the Black pioneers of civilization.

> *It is no secret that much of what parades as African have been interpreted only in the light of Europe, thus warping our understanding of theory and method...*
>
> *Unfortunately, the Africanists, much like Egyptologists, their counterparts who deal with ancient Egypt, tend to be Europeans whose interest in Africa serves European studies more than African studies.*[97]

Fortunately, as natural law would have it, many of the people who were trained were sincere and hard working, and therefore able to read more into what the research revealed. A good example is expressed in *The Healing Wisdom of Africa*, by Dr. Malidoma Patrice Some. He described Black and White people as one people at war against self.

> *...(I)ndigenous and western peoples are actually children of the same house they*

[97] Asante, Molefi Kete, *Pyramids of Knowledge* Brooklyn, NY: Universal Write Publications, 2015, p. 6, 7

> *call Earth. No matter what they do to torture each other, the dysfunctional relationship of modern and indigenous peoples is systematic to share love for each other that is deeply buried in our psyches, a craving so alive that it is compelled to struggle through the rubble of division, power conflicts, and fear to express itself.*[98]

Mr. Some was born in the Dagara tradition of Burkina Faso. His father named him "he who makes friends with the stranger/enemy." He was four years old when he was "stolen from one world and taken to another," to attend a French Catholic School, Dr. Some said in the book. He described himself as one of thousands of African children who were taken away from family and culture, and reared in a foreign culture. After completing general studies in the European tradition, he said, he returned to his village and family to study the indigenous tradition.

> *Because education was a departure from home and all its values, because it meant forgetting the ancestral ways in order to survive, education fostered in me and my colleagues a serious crisis of identity. When I returned to my village, the home I found was not in any way like home to me. Initially I could not accept that this was*

---

[98] Some, Malidoma Patrice. (1998). *The Healing Wisdom of Africa.* New York: Jeremy P. Tarcher/Putnam. p. 15.

> *the place of my birth. Faced with blatant uncleanliness, nakedness displayed without shame, and painfully unsophisticated dwellings, I began to pity my own people. Even worst, their lack of awareness of how backward, stagnant, and uncouth they were drove me to anger at the unfairness of God for associating me with them.*[99]

Fortunately, Dr. Some stayed, studied, and rediscovered the significance of his ancient traditions. His experience should be studied by people who go away from their own people to study with others. The plot thickened, however, when Dr. Some decided to return to the "West" to teach what he had learned from his people.

> *I found here in the West people who were so submerged in the massive trance of modern culture that they appeared to be virtually unreachable. It became clear that certain topics of discussion, such as spirituality and rituals, were not permitted in intellectual and professional circles... I am still recovering from the inflamed words of people who retaliated at me for referring to indigenous people as having power...*[100]

---

[99] Ibid., p. 7.
[100] Ibid., p. 14

Dr. Some's account of his experiences did not surprise me. He, in my opinion, needed THEM's teachings to understand the people who stole him from his culture and attempted to impose their own story on him. They resisted his mere mention of the fact that Indigenous cultures have power. The two people are at war. The original and the new people who were made in opposition to the status quote are engaged in an often times deadly battle I do not believe Mr. Some understands.

THEM was taught by Master Fard Muhammad (MFM), who studied the ancient archives of the Ottoman Empire before that empire was defeated (1918), least the invaders read and learn from said histories and gain a greater advantage.[101] Writers have since gone on to prove the history MFM taught THEM.

An example is found in the work of Paul Guthrie. In a book he titled: *Making of the Whiteman,* and dedicated to Minister Louis Farrakhan, he added to the evidence of the Teachings of THEM, that a people were made to oppose the original people.

> *"This (violent) change occurred in the area of the Caucasus Mountains. There, in West Asia, a previously unknown group of people suddenly appeared as if from out of nowhere. Collectively they are known as Indo-*

---

[101] Muhammad, Jesus Ali, *The Evolution of the Nation of Islam,* US: JMA Publishers, 2002, p. 13

> *European, Caucasians or white people. The facts show that they first entered the area around 6,000 years ago. (Two thousand) years later their invasions would bring them into contact with the civilized nations of the south.* [102]

The contact Mr. Guthrie referred to was well documented by Chancellor Williams in his book: *The Destruction of Black Civilization.*

> *The first period would begin with "prehistory," primarily because Nowe, one of the oldest cities on earth, was begun by Blacks before recorded history. Another important reason is that the Canaanites and Asians had invaded the Nile Delta and established a stronghold in Lower Egypt (then Northern Ethiopia or Chem) in prehistoric times. This early concentration of whites along the seacoast of the Land of Blacks is a circumstance of crucial importance in Black history because it was exactly from this development that the achievements of the Blacks were*

---

[102] Guthrie, Paul L. (1992). *Making of the Whiteman.* United States: Beacon Communications. p. 3

> *overshadowed by later writers or blotted out entirely...*
>
> *The second period might well be from the conquest of Lower Egypt by the Ethiopian leader, Menes, in 3100 B.C. to the end of the Sixth Dynasty, 2181, also the end of the Old Kingdom.*
>
> *This was the period that gave birth to Egypt, and before which there was no Egypt. It was the period during which black kings united the "Two Lands," started the dynastic (lineage) system, and began the building of the greatest civilization...* [103]

A series of invasions by (other Africans), Persians, Greeks, Romans, and Arabs followed, until African Arabs decided to invade Spain in 711 A.D. [104] Moors ruled that part of Europe until the African leader, Abu Abdi-Llah, otherwise known as Boabdil, was defeated by Spain and forced to surrender on January 2, 1492. The defeat of the African Moors in Spain led to "the massive burning of African and Arab books under the order of Cardinal Ximenes de Cisneros."[105]

---

[103] Williams, Chancellor. (1987). *The Destruction of Black Civilization.* Chicago: Third World Press. p. 39
[104] Van Sertima, Ivan. (1996). *The Golden Age of the Moors.* New Brunswick: Transaction Publishers. p. 1
[105] Ibid., p. 13

It also freed the Spanish Crown to finance Christopher Columbus' attempt to find a westward passage to the wealth of India and China. Although he never found what he was looking for, the bonfires of African and Arab books in Spain later "inspired a similar bonfire of the books of native Americas" by Bishop de Landa. He "exhorted his followers in the Yucatan 'Burn them all – they are works of the devil." [106]

Those bonfires, I believe, were designed to hide the true identity of the original Black settlers of the Americas, as so many of the authors this project has quoted from has said. In particular, the Empress, Rev. Amen-Ra, and Horace Butler spoke to a particular conspiracy that has been invented to hide the true history of the Americas. Each of them had a different spin but nevertheless described a desire to bury the truth.

The Filling In of the Blanks

As explained earlier, Columbus actually knew what he was looking for when he sailed down from Spain to the westward current Mr. Butler said Africans called the Jordan.[107] They had been using the natural current, which flows down from West Africa to Central America, for at least 10,000 years before the Christian Era.[108]

---

[106] Ibid., p. 13
107 Butler (2009) p. 123
108 Ibid, p. 16

Butler filled in the blanks for me when he described the wars that were waged by Africans against Africans in the Americas before others began to settle in the west where he said Moses was.

> *More than a history, the hieroglyphic record claimed to be a copy of an autobiography written by Moses....*
>
> *The autobiography implied that, after accidentally striking to death the Egyptian Pharaoh, Moses fled from Thebes, hurrying northward. The Bible had already told about that northward flight. But the Egyptian narrative named the place where Moses settled, "Peten."*
>
> *...Peten is a large important region at the southern end of the Yucatan Peninsula. Biblical accounts call this place, "Pithom."*
>
> *...According to the same Egyptian record of Moses, it was from Peten that Moses launched his great war, which the Bible calls an exodus.*
>
> *...Moses walked out of Peten with a massive army of more than 600,000 men. More than an exodus, Moses had planned a military invasion of Egypt!* [109]

---

[109] Ibid, p. 123, 124

Later, the writer actually discusses the modern day country of Belize in the narrative of Hebrews crossing the Jordan to make war with Egyptians in the Yucatan.

> *From his military base near Jericho, Joshua sent his warriors to attack a city called Ai. That was no small feat, as Ai is located on the Yucatan Peninsula; in the country we now call Belize. The Hebrews had to ply across a thousand miles of Atlantic and Caribbean seas to reach Ai...*
>
> *On maps that show ancient Maya cities, the Old Testament city, "Ai," seemed to be the Mayan city called "Ha," or "Altun Ha."*[110]

Butler continued to reveal some very interesting links to modern history, including the names of places in the Americas and in Africa.

> *The invasion and capture of Egypt's cities in the Americas, launched during the time of Joshua, eventually carved out an empire that included regions in Mexico, Central America, South America and West Africa.*
>
> *Descendants of Abraham's descendant "Jair" (Josh 13:30) were among the "two and a half tribes" settled in West Africa. It may be that this "Jair" is the reason Niger (Ni-Jair) and Nigeria (Ni-Jair-ia) have those names.*[111]

---
[110] Ibid, p. 158
[111] Ibid, p. 166

Butler showed, through records attributed to Herodotus, Columbus, Cortez, the Old Testament and other sources, arguments that baffle modern scholars. He revealed that the wars displaced the Egyptians from the Americas and some Hebrews went back to West Africa and some stayed in the west. He then suggested that the next group of people to enter the Americas was the Spanish who were determined to destroy the evidence of the builders of the first Egypt.

Of course, others would argue that the (Yellow) Chinese were next and then came the Spanish, as will be explained.

The Empress' Words Begin to Come to Life

The Late Empress of the Washitaw Nation had more to say on the subject of Black folks being erased from the history of the Americas. She said the first non- Black people to enter the Americas in large groups, was the (Yellow) Chinese, which is confirmed by the Gladwin Theory. (see Chapter 3/A) She said (Mongolian) Chinese walked across the Bering Strait and down into the northwest corner of North America until their numbers were great enough to push, kill and rape Black folks out from the centers of power. After they removed the Blacks, they claimed the cities, monuments, and the resources they knew to exploit for themselves before

Columbus ever reached the Americas. When White folks did arrive in great numbers they systematically attributed the evidence of civilization to the more aggressive ancient Mongolian type folks. In other words, the non-Black people you see in the Americas are European, Mongolian, or a combination of both. The aggressive and violent process, over time, according to THEM, rendered the first teachers on the planet, particularly in North America, "lost sheep" from the rest of our global family. His language is brutally raw, but he explained one the most sensitive issues facing human beings when he detailed the nature of Blacks and others.

> *Through the experimentation by the wicked slavemasters who were made without love or mercy for Black people, they have the Black man in America before the world as a wrecked, robbed, and spoiled human being without knowledge of himself or anyone else. And he is used by the white man as a tool for whatever purpose the white man sees fit.*[112]

The lesson most of the brilliant people I have quoted in this project never received what THEM taught. He said White people were made to hate, murder, and replace Black people by their Black father, Yakub.

---

[112] Muhammad, Elijah. (1974). *Our Saviour has Arrived.* Chicago: Muhammad's Temple #2. p. 99

The Purpose

Mr. Yakub, the White man's father was a wise scientist who was dissatisfied with his society, according to THEM. At age 6 he told his uncle he was going to make a new people to replace the Original rulers of the earth. By 16, he had graduated the universities of his day and managed to recruit 59,999 other dissatisfied members of his society. This happened 6,000 years ago.

I believe Butler described the type of warfare and disrespect the original people of the earth were living under. There must have been a cast system that produced envy, jealousy, hatred and murder among Black people on this planet. I believe the wealthy and wise were able to travel the seas and enjoy the Americas for a time. THEM taught his followers that a rebellious group was exiled to the Americas 16,000 years ago. They were forced to walk through the Bering Strait and down into the Americas. Others, as Butler explained, traveled the Oceans by boats.

By the time Yakub was born, 10,000 years after the rebellious people had been exiled from the east into the west, he made, not created, a new people.

In order to flesh out that idea, after travel, interviews, research and writing, I was guided to San Antonio, Texas, to interview one of my first teachers, a longtime

Nation of Islam Study Group Coordinator, Brother J.D. Muhammad. I also visited the sacred grounds of the Alamo while there.

Brother J.D. described the Black man's sojourn in the Americas as a designed process and eventual purging.

"The Messenger (THEM) taught us that God permitted us to suffer in the Americas in order to erase qualities within the Original man that actually produced the White man from the 'dissatisfied' of our ancient society. The murderer we see in White people came from Black people. The purpose of White and Yellow people being permitted to invade Black cultures was to show the original man something inside himself he would not be able to see otherwise.

"He said the lesson was designed to show that we must learn to master the weakness or devil inside of ourselves, which is expressed in the hostility many Black people experience in the world. When we learn to lock the devil down on the inside of ourselves, the one on the outside becomes easy to subdue." [113]

The biggest questions, of course, are why does God permit the rebellion against truth and when will it end? These are the questions I wanted to leave on the minds of the folks I met in Cuajinicuilapa and those who read this project.

---

[113] Muhammad, JD interview at his home., 2007

The most important lesson, I believe, is that the historical enemies of Black people or the original man and woman did not fall from the sky. They were produced from the ways we treated each other in a distant past and the ways we continue to treat each other. As THEM taught, Black people produced a new and angry people from the dissatisfied (with society).

The Final Revelation

Once again, I thought I was done until I ran into Bro. Islam Shabazz Allah on the Nile (125th Street in Harlem). He told me he was reading *Annihilation of Caste*, by B.R. Ambedkar, with a 124 page introduction by Arundhati Roy.

By the time I read the introduction, which exposed Mohandas Karamchand Gandi as a racist, and introduced me to the writer of the book who rose from the "Untouchable caste" to become Dr. Bhimrao Ramji Ambedkar, a graduate of Columbia University, I realized why Gandi was loved by those who write history. The final revelation that dawned on me is that White people were members of the Untouchable class in a distant past. They were "dissatisfied," as THEM explained. He said the White man was made from original people from India a little over 6,000 years ago. The Hindu system is much older but it was never based on color but on what your parents did. This project has already discussed the fact that enslaved human beings existed in Africa long before it existed in Europe, but as explained by Cheikn Anta Diop, it was different. Mr. Diop wrote in *Precolonial Black Africa,* that the slave owners had a obligation to the poor. "The Fondoko Borom, 'Lord of the Macina' (1610) thought that any person invested with royal authority was the servant and shepherd of his people."[114]

Diop not only separated Africa from the caste system in India, even though he agreed it started in Africa, but blamed the difference on the invasion of the Aryan in India approximately 35,000 years ago.

> *Giving a divine character to property is an Aryan custome: in Rome, Greece, and India it led to isolation from society of an entire category of individuals who had no family, had neither health nor home, and no right of ownership. They would everywhere constitute the class of the wretched...which had not been forseen by the traditional and sacred laws regulating ownership that were made up by the ancestors of the Aryans.*[115]

Gandi, on the other hand, loved the Hindu system and refererred to it, according to Ms. Roy, as "the genius of Indian society."[116]

---

[114] Diop, Cheikh Anta *Precolonial Black Africa*, Lawrence Hill Books (1987) p. 63
[115] Ibid, p. 13
[116] Ambedkar, B.R., *Annihilation of Caste*, 2014, Brooklyn, NY, p. 25

THEM and his teacher, Master Fard Muhammad (MFM), hated the Hindu system.

> *Hindus have been on this planet for untold ages. They are an original people. They have been here for a long, long time. For 35,000 years, they have been worshipping other than the real God...*
> *He is far worse than any religious person you know of.*[117]

The Hindu system is based on four varnas (Caste groups in Hindu India that are associated with certain occupations) from the body of primeval man. Gandi was a Bania (Vaishyas), as opposed to the highest caste. Although he defended the system he was third down in the system.

> *The highest caste, the Brahmins (priests and scholars), came from his mouth; the Kshatrivas (warriors) emanated from his arms; the Vaishyas (tradsmen) came from his thighs; and the Shudras (cultivators and servants) sprang from his feet.*
> *Each of these four castes is hierarchically ranked according to its ritual purity.*
> *Below these four castes-and technically outside the caste system-is still another category, called the Untouchables or, literally outcastes.*[118]

---
[117] Muhammad, (1974), p. 32
[118] Cultural Anthropology: *An Applied Perspective, 10th Edition*, Gary Ferraro and Susan Andreatta, 2014, Cengage Learning, USA, p. 302

Ms. Roy described the Untouchables or Dalit (Broken People) in words Ambedkar used in a speech he was to deliver to "priviledged-caste Hindus" in 1936 at Lahore, India. The speech was never delivered because he refused to change parts of it that would have offended the Hindus. "Hinduism is veritable chamber of horrors," she quoted Ambedkar as saying in the introduction.

> *According to the National Crime Records Bureau, a crime is committed against a Dalit by a non-Dalit every sixteen minutes; every day, more than four Untouchable women are raped by Touchables; every week, thirteen Dalits are murdered and six Dalits are kidnapped. In 2012 alone, the year of the Delhi gang-rape and murder, 1574 Dalit women were raped (the rule of thumb is that only 10 percent of rapes or \other crimes against Dalits are ever reported),and 651 Dalits were murdered.*[119]

Taken from the text of the speech Ambedkar was to deliver to the prominent Hindus in 1936 follows

> *Under the rule of the Peshwas in the Maratha country, the Untouchable was not allowed to use the public streets if a Hindu was coming along, lest he should polute the Hindu by his shadow.*

[119] Ambedkar, (2014), p. 21

> *The Untouchable was required to have a black thread either on his wrist or around his neck, as a sign or a mark to prevent the Hindus from getting themselves polluted by his touch by mistake. In Poona, the capital of the Peshwa, the Untouchable was required to carry, strung around his waist, a broom to sweep away from behind himself the dust he trod on, lest a Hindu walking on the same dust should be polluted. In Poona, the Untouchable was required to carry an earthen pot around his neck wherever he went-for holding his spit, lest his spit falling on the earth should pollute a Hindu who might unknowingly happen to tread on it.*[120]

The reading helped me to understand why THEM said "if the Hindu and the Christian are walking together, (Master Fard Muhammad said,) "kill the Hindu first because the Hindu is more poisonous than the Christian."[121]

The Western world, in my opinion, is based on the Hindu concept of caste. One does what their parents did. The good thing about the White and Yellows' "determined idea of hatred and murder" of the original man, to replace him, is that it has proven the whole myth of superiority to be wrong. The people who were once on the bottom are now on top.

[120] Ambedkar, (2014), p. 214
[121] Muhammad, (1974), p. 32, 33

Suddenly, *Egyptian Sacred Science in Islam* began to help my so-called revelation. I recalled reading about the "untouchables" from another angle that pointed to White people or cultures that promote the eating of pork.

> *The religion of ancient Egypt and the religion of Al- Islam also share certain practices:*
>
> *1) Ancient Egyptians practiced a 30-day fast. Likewise, the Muslims fast for 30 days each year in commemoration of the Qur'anic revelations. This month of thankful-ness and cleansing is called Ramadan*
>
> *2) Ancient Egyptians had an abhorrence to pork and only consumed it once a year in a special ceremony. Set, the name of the evil principle, was often depicted as a pig. Even swineherdsmen were strictly avoided untouchables. Further, Ancient Egyptians neither kissed Greeks nor ate from Greek utensils because the Greeks consumed pork. Muslims are enjoined not to eat pork at all and Muslims are known as a religious body of people which exhibits strict adherence to this practice.*[122]

---

[122] Bilal, Goodman, (1985), p. 16

I found the above quote to confirm that Christian or White nations embrace the eating of pork a wish to impose the practice on others. Please note that people were referred to as "swineherders" who "were strictly avoided untouchables" in the above quote.

The prophesied Resurrection of the Dead, finally, will not be contingent on which political party or religion the dead Black man and woman chooses. We who are dead or have no political, financial, spiritual power or unity must learn to stop jockeying for advantage over one another. We must adjust our appreciation for each other and chose cooperation as opposed to competition.

God is not really punishing us. He is demanding that we, the oldest rebels on earth, learn to assist one another. That is the message I have heard from teachers but have come to understand while striving to complete this pledge.

Minister Farrakhan explained to an audience some years ago that the family of God (the Dead) must return home, but not to a particular place on our planet, like Africa, as many of us believe, for example. A return home, he said, is a return to the Mind of God.

I believe that to be the answer we all have been searching for. That idea may prove to be the answer to all of the questions this project has raised…

STATEMENT OF PURPOSE AND METHODOLOGY

"Everywhere others have traveled the earth, (they have discovered that) Black people have already been there."

-Elijah Muhammad

Black Mexico: The Greatest Story Never Told

Black man, know thyself

A child stands in front of a stone sculpture of the face of a Mayan god found at the base of Maya ruins at Lamani in Belize. This and other ruins found in Central and South America verifies the Black man's presence in the Americas long before Columbus. See page 35 for details.

[From the Final Call (1994). Photo Credit, Lamont Muhammad]

A Statement of Purpose and Methodology

The First Light

The roots of this project began in 1965, when I pledged to a Harlem based Fraternity called The Order of the Feather (TOOF), a Harlem based Fraternity under the auspices of Camp Minisink and the New York City Mission Society. Pledgees were required to read *Before the Mayflower,* by Lerone Bennett. I now believe the experience of reading and discussing the book, at age 16, set me on a course for seeking and documenting hidden Black History. I was pleasantly surprised to find the book exciting. Suddenly I found a desire to read more Black history. I was no longer resistant to reading as I once had been when I was required to read edited versions of Contemporary (Euro) History. I had discovered historical narratives that were relevant to my experience. The stories or accounts I read in Mr. Bennett's book helped to quench a thirst I had for meaning. Among the tidbits the book revealed to me was the fact that Egypt is in Africa, and that Cleopatra was an African Queen. That was news to me. I had never been taught that history in those terms. The White actress Elizabeth Taylor was the Cleopatra I was familiar with.

Subsequently, of course, I did learn that Cleopatra was relatively a new (type) African. She represented the 5th generation of imposed rule after "Alexander the Great" invaded Egypt (332 B.C.) and eventually gave the conquered territory to one of his generals, Ptolemy I Soter (305-285 B.C.). Nevertheless, learning that Egypt was in Africa hooked me onto the fields of history, anthropology, and archeology in an intrinsically motivated drive to read, research, and to discover the hidden history of Black people.

Later (1967), I was accepted to Queens College in New York and pledged to the Order of the Black Enlightenment. The idea in the heads of the founders was to distance ourselves from the Greek Fraternities or "The Divine Nine," which were the Fraternities that had Greek names and rituals that were secret. Pledgees were required to lecture Black High School groups around the city with the truth about our Black selves during the turbulent 1960's.

By January, 1970, I dropped out of school and joined the army during the Viet Nam War (1970 to 1972). If the streets of the South Bronx and Harlem had not killed me, what did South East Asia have that could, I figured. I was very confused by the times.

I was stationed in Japan (five months) and Thailand (nine months). I spent 20 minutes in the Saigon Airport because no G.I. was allowed off of the plane there unless Vietnam was his or her destination. The experience in Asia represented my first exposure to ancient cultures outside of the United States. I believe I spent more time off base with the natives than I spent on base with the G.I.s It was also the first time I got to recognized little difference between the Brown (Asian) people I saw in Thailand (especially), and the Brown (Latin) people I had seen and met in the Americas.

Although I had signed up for a four-year stretch in the Army, I got out in 1972 (1 year and 11 months) and moved to Atlanta because I had heard Black millionaires lived there. I did love the city but found myself leaving it for New York (1974) and eventually Boston because I had friends there in school.

In 1975 or so I met a Black Puerto Rican student at Boston's Northeastern University who was from New York. He turned me onto *The Dramatic Prophesies of the Great Pyramid,* by Rodolfo Benavides. The book took me to another level. It helped to understand to better understand the relationship between Mexico and Kemet. It interpreted Benavides' view of what that relationship represents through the symbols he said they left in stone and the imaginations of those who would study. He described the current state of human affairs as part of a process toward another ultimate reality. The book became a bible that guided me through counseling and teaching positions in Boston. My job sent me to a conference in Chicago where I visited the Institute of Positive Education, the Du Sable Museum and the Oriental Institute at the University of Chicago. I was set. I subsequently established the Institute of Cultural Education (ICE) and the Order of Cultural Enlightenment (OCE) in Boston (1977) before I left for New York (1979).

Finally, between the wisdom I had gained and my confusion about what was going on, I submitted my world to the Addicts Rehabilitation Center (ARC) in Harlem. As I taught the information I had learned about Kemet, which at the time I called Egypt, I began to hear Minister Louis Farrakhan explain the teachings of the Honorable Elijah Muhammad (THEM). I immediately understood the message. It confirmed the messages I had received when I pledged to the TOOF, and THEM's message helped me to better understand what Mr. Benavides and the other pioneer writers I had been reading were saying. I was slowly beginning to discover the real contributions Black people had made to modern civilization. I also began to see that the evidence had been buried by those who had invaded and robbed the people who had formed the foundation of high culture. I was learning to see my crippled people as victims of greed and "a determined idea of hatred and murder," as THEM said.

By 1980, I was beginning to realize that my experience in the public sector (which was controlled and financed by corporate America) had been designed to keep me poor and ineffective. I was already a community organizer (Minisink), a teacher (Minisink, ICE, OCE) and I was becoming a journalist (Graduate of Trans Urban News Internship, 1980), but I was still poorly paid, somewhat unconscious, and relegated to the margins of American society.

Nevertheless, it was that year, after listening to Minister Farrakhan resurrecting the teachings of THEM and reading the Final Call since 1979, that I decided to accept the message. I decided to completely dedicate my skills to the resurrection of Black people. My last job in the public sector was directing a youth (business) training program on the Lower East Side of New York. After securing less funding for a second year, I tendered my resignation and became a freelance journalist with the Black Press.

In 1983, I moved away from New York to accept an invitation from a friend in Indianapolis (Nap), Indiana. She told me she was friends with two people who owned Black newspapers there. I worked for the Indianapolis Recorder for $1 a column inch. I also wrote for Indianapolis Visions Magazine, and organized for the Nation of Islam (NOI) there. I soon discovered, however, that I could barely make a living there as a reporter unless I worked for White owned newspapers with White or White minded editors.

In 1985, I decided to leave "Nap Town" and to return to the vibrant East Coast. As I drove on I-70, which at the time ran from my back door in Nap and ended in Baltimore, my destination, much was happening. It was Mother's Day weekend. The Philadelphia Police Department dropped a bomb on the MOVE organization and a celebrated football team in Baltimore secretly moved to Indianapolis. When I arrived in Baltimore I read an editorial in the Baltimore Afro-American Newspaper that was critical of Min. Farrakhan. I wrote an article to the editor there in the Minister's defense and was offered a job. I took it and also met an intern there whom I eventually married. Paula Wagner Robinson's dream, she explained to me, was to acquire an English degree from the University of Maryland, and to return to her "Black, independent, English speaking nation on the shores of the Caribbean Sea, Belize in Central America." I said: "Let's go," before ever seeing the place.

We got married and moved to Belize for two years that first time. We were also blessed with a baby for each of those two years. Belize is where I was first exposed to the ancient ruins and cultures of Central America, and Mexico.

We left Belize and returned to Baltimore in 1989. By now, of course, I couldn't get the little Kemet I had seen in Belize out of my mind, which stayed on the similarities between the pyramids I had seen in Central America and Mexico, and those I had only scene in books and on television about Kemet (Egypt). I was also gaining a better understanding of what Mr. Benavides had written and what THEM had said to his Believers and the world. After nearly three years and an additional two babies that were born in Baltimore, Paula decided to return to Belize with the children to teach school and to get away from her deadbeat husband. Although I tried to support my family, I couldn't find a descent way to support them and to fulfill what I believed to be my calling.

They left me and I stayed in Baltimore until I was eventually hired to cover the United Nations (UN) in New York, by *The Final Call*. My beat was Africa, the Caribbean, and developing nations. I was also back in the city in which I was born with my mother, who was suffering with cancer.

Between the job and visiting my family in Belize – two to three times a year – I traveled around North America, including Mexico; and visited Kemet while practicing journalism.

In 1996 my mother returned to the Lord of the Worlds and left me, her only child, the gift of her labors and sacrifice. My family and I had decided to get back together before my mother joined the realm of the ancestors – but her untimely return to the Source helped to push the reunion along. My family was back in the US while I continued my commitment to the *Final Call*. After the "World's Day of Atonement," at the UN (October, 1996), I was free to find a replacement and to go after my intrinsic mission or dream.

Ancient Geographic Expression Systems (AGES) is Born

My family and I went to Africa to get reacquainted. I had never forgotten the report by another Believer that a combination of blood and feces still lined the floors of the castles that were built by the Portuguese where the enslaved Africans were held. "You can still smell it," he said.

It was true, the smell of those tragic events remained. There, against the fishing boats the locals still used and the other cultural realities that remained, my children were at home there. Having been nurtured in Belize, they were able to translate the English the Ghanaians spoke for me. I would've been clueless without them. I discovered that the various Caribbean accents were actually African accents. My children also understood the fruit trees and the grasses because subtropical Belize was very similar. However, I soon discovered, everything in Ghana was bigger. The experience convinced me and Paula agreed, to move them back to Belize where the children were more familiar and where they were receiving a superior formal education, as we saw it.

We moved back to Belize that year (1996) and we also established Ancient Geographical Expressions Systems (AGES). It was incorporated in Delaware and later in Belize. AGES Publishing Company was dedicated to documenting the African foundation of world civilizations.

Unfortunately, in 1997, Paula and I had problems and she returned to the U.S. with our children and I stayed in a big house in Belize by myself for three additional years with a determination to make my publishing company work. I continued to travel the country but in October 1998, I decided to follow the advice of a friend in Belize. Stretch Lightburn, as I explained in the Acknowledgments, told me to go document the existence of the Black people in the market center village of Cuajinicuilapa, Mexico.

I hired a Muslim translator in Belize whose father was a Black man who was born in Belize and whose mother was an indigenous Guatemalan. He spoke English and Spanish, and he knew Mexico. Brother Adam Banks Muhammad was my guide from Belize to Mexico and across her Southwestern Valley to Cuajinicuilapa, and back to the Mexico/Belize border. In between, he translated conversations, interviews, provided context, and generally demystified the different cultures for me during the 10 day contract.

It was an eye opening experience to see the many Black people who lived in Acapulco, but I was to see more as I traveled south to the Costa Chica, which I have discussed extensively in Chapter One.

In 2000, I published the pamphlet edition of *Black Mexico: The Greatest Story Never Told (Black Mexico)*. I left Belize to return to the US and to spread the word about the Black folks that I had met in Mexico.

The Latest Edition

I touched down in the US in Phoenix, Arizona, with the help of Sister Valerie E. Muhammad, who also introduced me to two other members of the Nation of Islam. Fortunately, they also considered themselves Muurs and were membersof an organization called the Nation of the Washitaw de Dugdahmoundyah. Brother, Dr. Gregory Muhammad, and his nephew, Bro. Seth Muhammad demystified the connection between that Nation and the history of the Americas.

Eventually, Bro. Seth and I drove from Phoenix to Reston, Louisiana to meet Her Highness Verdiacee Tiari Washitaw – Turner Goston El-Bey, the Empress of the Ancient American culture and author of *The Return of the Ancients*. In interviews that ran for three-days, the Empress began to demystify the demographic landscape of the Americas for me, as we explain in *Appendix A*.

Next, I journeyed to New York City, by way of Baltimore. In Harlem, the late Sister Pah'Ti, a friend and dress maker for many, liked *Black Mexico*, and gave me a copy of *The Forgotten Truth Behind Racism in America: The Hidden Identity of the Black American Vol. 1*, by Reverend Amen-Ra. The book described "Black American Mound Builders" as refugees from North Africa who were instructed by God to leave Africa before the Great Flood. The information began to teach me to look at the ancient Black cultures of the Americas differently.

Next I ran into an old friend who had been born in Haiti and migrated with his family to the U.S. when he was a child. Yaw attempted to introduce me to Vooduun. I attended a few ceremonies but I felt that I was being tested for a mission he had in mind. My Haitian brother was introducing me, as I saw it, to a new mission. Little did I understand at the time that the Haitian history was an untold story of Blacks in general. It wasn't time for me. I was driven to stay on my own (perceived) course.

During that period, a Biology teacher named Dr. Jack Felder, invited me to his school to talk to his (Junior High School) students and others about *Black Mexico*. He later introduced me to Linda Fletcher, an Anthropologist and an advocate for (resurrection) organizations in Belize and other places. Her work introduced me to the academic world's definitions of what we were doing and to the on the ground concept of Anthropology. She was first to call me a Socio- Anthropologist.

In late August, 2001, while starting this 2nd edition, and listening to Radio Station WBAI, I heard a reference to two women who had traveled eight-days by bus from Oaxaca, Mexico to New York to attend an Indigenous Conference at the UN. They were in studio there. One was described as a light skinned Indian and the other, a dark skinned African-Mexican. I immediately turned the radio up. I called into the station and they invited me to meet them. When I arrived they invited me and others to some of the engagements they had planned to attend around the city. I was impressed with their determination, both the African and the so-called Indian, to inform the outside world of the challenges Black Mexicans face in Oaxaca, Mexico.

Maria Callejas Salinas described Mexico as a bastion of White Supremacy that ignores Black people "simply because we are Black." The words of her colleague, Patricia Pena, helped my bottom line when she said, representing the Chatino Nation in Oaxaca: "There had to be another people (in my village) before my people. We don't make floors and doors." In other words, there was a previous civilization there that used floors and doors. That civilization was more advanced than they were, she explained.

Later, in October, 2001, I was asked to write a three-part series on the Sea Islands, from Amelia Island, off of the coast of Jacksonville, Florida. While there I met the Gullah/Geechee people. They, who lived on the islands that run from Florida to South Carolina, were described as a people who still practice African traditions. In fact, the movie *"Daughters of the Dust,"* depicted generations of one family from there that was divided into those who wanted to stay and maintain African traditions and others who wanted to leave the island because they believed the island life was backwards. The movie, beautifully shot on St. Helena, one of the Sea Islands, was the actual story of Julie Dash's family. She wrote the independent film, directed and produced it in 1991. It was about some of her family who left the island in 1902. I did meet some Gullah people who still practice African traditions during my trip and assignment there.

On one of my two trips back to Belize to get some of items I had left there, I began to see what folks had been telling me about the history of the area when I looked into the face of a friend. She was an organizer for the Maya in Belize. I could see the Chinese features in her face. Her son had curly hair and her daughter had straight hair. Suddenly, I was beginning to understand the words of the Empress. I was beginning to understand that the Chinese not only found pyramids in Mexico and Central America, but they found and conquered Black people, assumed their identity and the monuments that still remain in the region. The discovery helped me to understand the hidden parts of our history.

When I returned to New York, I moved from my adopted new home in Brooklyn back to Harlem where I was comfortable. I moved to a room and eventually called Professor James Small to discuss the Chinese role in the progression of Black history in the Western Hemisphere. He agreed to meet me for breakfast on the hill in Harlem. When we hooked up the next morning, I told him about my project and about my experiences in Central America. When I asked him about the Chinese role in American history he deferred to retired New York Public School Assistant Principal and former art major, Ego Hayes. That meeting and information has been detailed in Chapter three.

At the time, I was freelancing as a journalist and volunteering at a Black bookstore on Adam Clayton Powell Boulevard. The store was owned by a friend and Believer, Brother Lester Muhammad. I was not only back in Central Harlem, but I was surrounded by the great books I needed to read (having left many of my own back in Belize) to round out my pledge to the Mexicans I had met in Cuajinicuilapa.

Simultaneously, as God would have it, the William Morrow Publishing House was pushing a new writer, Gavin Menzies, author of *1421: The Year China*

Discovered America. I was so eager to get a review copy that I called a William Marrow representative a number of times to complain that I hadn't received one. By the time I did finally receive one – I received another copy the following day. I gave a copy to Mr. Hayes, and by the time Mr. Menzies was doing his book launch at the Asia Society House in New York, Hayes had briefed me and I was ready, as I have already detailed.

Later, I read Runoko Rashidi's *Men Out of Asia: A review and Update of the Gladwin Thesis*. It was published in a compilation edited by Ivan Van Sertima, *African Presence in Early America* (1992). I found the paper enlightening. It began to demystify the process and to help me understand what the Empress was attempting to explain to me about the history of the Americas. She did say that she was taught by her grandmother, who was the Empress at the time, that the Chinese walked into the Americas and waited in the Northwestern part of the North America until their numbers were such that they could sweep down, run us from the centers of power and claim our history.

The Summary Process

When I initially sat down to close-out my pledge to the folks I had met in Cuajinicuilapa, I was somewhat confused. I was beginning to see White and Yellow folks as the manifestations of the banishments, intolerances, and the outright arrogance some Black people brought to the table many years ago, but I didn't know how to say it. I could see that we were responsible for the condition we were or are in. The words of Minister Farrakhan were coming to light. He said that we are the oldest rebels against the Words of Almighty God, Allah, on earth and we will continue to suffer until we wakeup. When I shopped the idea with my friends, to test my new ideas, I was met with resistance and hostility.

"You mean Black folks suffer 'cause we got problems, within? The White man ain't in it? Nigga, please," a good friend in Baltimore said to me. My friends treated my idea as if I did not understand history, or how difficult life is for Black people today under White people's civilization, especially for those who want to be their own Black selves. That is when I realized I needed more evidence to make my argument more convincing and clear. I decided to return to Ego Hayes and to share my problem with him. When I suggested that Black folks are dealing with a type of karma or payback from prior relations with each other, he agreed.

"Africans have been making enemies a long time," he explained during that interview. "Kings in ancient Africa were known to banish whole groups from the society in order to keep some groups ignorant and therefore useful tools of service to the king and his family in the future," he said.

Have you read, *Pre-colonial Black Africa*, by Dr. Cheikh Anta Diop? He asked. I bought the book the next day.

> *In Senegal, society is divided into slaves and freedmen, the latter being gor, including both ger and neno...*
> *But - and herein lay the real originality of the system-unlike the attitude of the nobles toward the bourgeoisie, the lords toward the serfs, or the Brahmans toward the other Indian castes, the ger could not materially exploit the lower castes without losing face in the eyes of others, as well as their own. On the contrary, they were obliged to assist lower caste members in every way possible: even if less wealthy, they had to "give" to a man of lower caste if so requested. In exchange, the latter had to allow them social precedence.*[123]

That model can stand for "the whole of detribalized Sudanese Africa," Dr. Diop wrote. African caste systems, he argued, are the oldest on earth.

Diop's words substantiated the teachings of Mr. Muhammad for me. They showed how an ancient idea that was designed to serve all can morph into pockets of dissatisfaction. In time, permanent social structures

---

[123] Diop, Cheikh Anta. *Pre-colonial Black Africa*, Lawrence Hill Books (1987), pg. 2

breed resentment, bitterness, hatred, and murder in the minds of people like Mr. Yakub.

In 2007 I received an email from a good friend and fellow journalist who covered the UN a lot longer than I had, Joy Elliott. The message was looking for Journalists for a Red Cross press junket to Benin, West Africa, with Sidney Poitier. I applied and was accepted for the 9 day trip. It was my third trip to the Motherland.

Fortunately or unfortunately, I was so caught up in the celebrity of Sidney Poitier, the plight of the Africans the trip was organized to inoculate, and my commitment to writing the stories for the newspapers I said I would that I got lost in the mix.

After that trip I had more questions than answers. I was stuck in the "valley of decision," as followers of Mr. Muhammad say. The condition continued for years until I was accepted into a Veteran's Rehab program and soon after enrolled at the College of New Rochelle (2010).

School returned my enthusiasm for study, organizing my findings, and writing them out, thanks to Almighty God, Allah.

Finally, as I was winding down from my research and closing out this book, I was told by a close friend and brother, Ray Muhammad, to read *When Rocks Cry Out*, by Horace Butler. He described the Aztecs as "dark skinned," including Montezuma (really called

Motecuhzoma), and accused the Spanish, led by Cortez, of attempting to destroy the evidence of what Africans had contributed to civilization.

> *One morning it dawned on me that Mexico is still governed by a people who arrived from Spain. Maybe Mayanists and other historians have no choice but to censure, censor, and erase the pre-Columbian African presence. But that is not certain. What is certain is that scholars who want to work at the pre-Columbian ruins in Mexico, Central American and South America often must get permission from Spanish Administrators in those countries...*
>
> *If there was no motive to deny the pre-Columbian African presence, why would a University professor deny an African presence in pre-Columbian America then whisper in notes at the back of his published book that the rulers of some of the most important Maya nations called themselves "black rulers?"*[124]

Butler's information reminded me of the many times I had offered to write about the area for airlines that fly to Mexico and Central America. My idea was that Black folks did not have to spend so much money to fly to Kemet. They could fly to the Maya region and see the same Pyramids as I had. I believed I would attract many people to the hidden idea or secret.

[124] Butler, p.44

Time after time the airlines folks would deny me. Butler, despite the fact that many reject his research, was beginning to help me understand the big secret. The wise do not want Black people to wakeup to the fact that Black people were the first to settle and rule the Americas. Finally, I was turned onto *The Annihilation of Caste*, as explained in "My Research," which helped me to see or believe where White folks got their model to keep us down. While reading the book and discussing it with others, a good friend gave me a copy of *The Africans Who Wrote The Bible: Ancient Secrets Africa and Christianity Have Never Told*, by Nana Banchie Darkwah, Ph.D. The book shed light on some of the things Horace Butler was saying, but I am not going to list the things he pointed out in the book. I will quote the back page and a few sentences from Chapter one of the lengthy books.

The back page says:

> *The greatest secret Africa has never told and Christian Europe has been seeking to conceal for the past two thousand years is the African origin of the concept, doctrines, sacramental practices of religion, and the documents that became the foundations of Christianity in Europe. It was from this fact that the Catholic Church got the Black Madonna, the Black mother of Jesus Christ...*

That was less than half of what the back page said. The following excerpt is from Chapter One:

> *...if the Jewish people are not Europeans or English people how did the authors of the New Testament come to be called by the English names Matthew, Mark, Luke and John that are not Jewish names? How did the cousin of Jesus come to be called John the Baptist, an English name, when he was not a European and specifically when he was not an Englishman? How did the disciples of Jesus acquire English names like Simon, Peter, Andrew, Philip, Bartholomew, Thomas, Matthew, James, Judas and others when these people were not English men, and when these names were not Jewish names either?[125]*

Mr. Darkwah's book was included in this essay because so many of the readers are so-called Christians, although many would argue that Black Christianity had morphed into a new identity.

> *For black writers of the eighteenth century, a Christian identity became a way to challenge slavery. The "democratization of American Christianity" in its forms and style of worship resulted in the growth of a distinct African American Christianity. Blacks began the long process of making Christianity their own, developing a liberation theology that identified with the enslaved Israelites as the chosen people of God and the story of Exodus.[126]*

---

[125] Darkwah, Nana Banchie, *The Africans Who Wrote the Bible,* White Plains, MD: An Aduana Publishing Book, 2005 p. 1

[126] Sinha, Manisha, the Slaves Cause: A History of Abolition, New Haven, CT: Yale University Press, p. 28

The inclusion was designed to give the reader more information to think about. Obviously, Black people have not been cursed, but challenged to look at self. THEM said Black or Original people would be identified as the disrespected people on the lowest level of living in this temporary world by Almighty God/Allah. He would visit and raise the people on the bottom to a level above Original people's open enemies. He would educate the Original people to treat each other better and therefore set up the Kingdom of God in North America, first. That number of New People would eventually include the Original people of the Caribbean; South, and Central America and then go out to the rest of the world.

I am thankful for the revelation, in my opinion, that White people were the originally dissatisfied people (swine herders) who wanted to replace the Originals with a determined idea. I believe this message frees the people I pledged this message to from an imposed sense of guilt and opens a window on who we really are and what we must do to grow into a new reality...

Think that over!!!

Thank you for reading these few words...

APPENDICES

APPENDIX A

The Original Americans were Black Muurs?
By Lamont Muhammad
12.27.00

Her Highness Verdiacee Tiari Washitaw – Turner Goston El-Bey, is the 73-year-old Empress of the Washitaw de Dugdahmoundyah, one of the oldest Indigenous nations to be found anywhere in the earth, say her followers and other reviewers at the United Nations (UN). She reigns over conscious descendants of the Muurs or Moundbuilders of the massive ancient ruins that dart the most significant points on the upper and lower parts of the Americas, the Empress explained.

Her Highness Verdiacee Tiari Washitaw –Turner Goston El-Bey. Photo by Lamont Muhammad

Invasions from Asia and Europe over recent centuries have uprooted her people from all but 68,883 acres of northern Louisiana. But, on paper her people own more, according to the UN, the United States (US) government, and the State of Louisiana. But the official recognitions have no teeth to enforce property rights of the

[Photo of the Empress of the Washitaw, who was hospitalized at the time in Louisiana. Author gave her a copy of the first edition of Black Mexico...]

current home and business owning settlers on Washitaw lands in Louisiana. The Empress wants them to pay rent to Washitaw or flee the land. Therefore, she, like the US Marines, "is looking for a few good men."

"We must reclaim land our Nation can recall our own," said Seth Muhammad, the young Washitaw organizer who helped arrange an exclusive interview between Her Highness and this writer in Reston, Louisiana, in June 2000.

The Empress is herself author of *The Return of the Ancient Ones* and her struggle is one of many afoot in the Western Hemisphere to reclaim land by way of litigation in the courtrooms of the invader/settler. Others are buying land and claiming sovereign status within specific frameworks defined by national and international protocols. They argue that the entire earth is home to the original family. They do not recognize borders. In addition, they do not believe all Black people in the Americas were brought in slave ships.

"We been here," declared the Empress, explaining that the original Native Americans were mostly of a dark complexion. She said the light-skin Indians of

Hollywood fame were minority tribes in the Northwest that were mixed with the blood of Chinese invaders.

"They made up less than a third of the total population of Indians on this land. White folks don't owe Black people in America 40 acres and a mule. They need to get up off our land or start paying us some rent and taxes," she said. Her argument is supported by Reverend RaDine Amen-ra, author of *The Forgotten Truth Behind Racism in America: The Hidden Ancestral Identity of the Black American Vol. I, (2000)*.

Reverend Amen-Ra describes the "Black American Mound Builders" that others call Indians, as people of the book. They are the Children of Israel, mentioned in the second book of the Pentateuch and the second book of the Bible, Exodus, she said. Her people, she explained, "were instructed by God to leave North Africa (Egypt) for a new homeland before the great flood which separated the continents."

> *The Mound Builders is the name given to the civilization of Nations ofthe largest indigenous group of people inhabiting North America. These people built over 250 thousand earthen-shaped pyramids over the last 12,000 years on the eastern portion of North and South America and islands. This vast civilization and their people mysteriously Vanished during the 1700's.*[127]

---

[127] Amen-ra, Reverend RaDine. (2000) *The Forgotten Truth Behind Racism in America: The Hidden Ancestral Identity of the Black American Vol.* Georgia: Quantum Leap Publications. p. 21

The author describes herself as an Indigenous American, born and raised by a Chickasaw mother and a Cherokee/Yamesse father in Westbury, New York. She argues in her book that less than three percent of the North American slaves came from villages in Africa. Most of the slaves in bondage in the U.S. were stolen as children from the North and Southeastern Nations of Mound Builders, she argued. When they caught a young adult in New Jersey, for example, they would put him on a ship for South Carolina.

"There they would be processed as a Negro into the plantation system."[128] They captured and traded most of our people from North, Central, South America, and the West Indies, not Africa, she repeated. They killed those who knew the truth and instilled fear and confusion in the unknowing children who survived and became dead (to their history) negroes.

> *How did the European Educational system create a slave mentality among today's Black Americans?*
>
> *By omitting the true story of how the early Colonialists acquired the land and, by keeping the true racial identity of the Indigenous American people, termed Indian, invisible. This omission created an inferiority complex within the psyche of the real American children. The result is as*

adults, they internalize in their heart that they owe someone else for their right to belong to America, with no respectable place of belonging within humanity. They accept their new position as sharecroppers in a foreign land, instead of knowing they are a people under siege by a constant invasion of foreign people in their homeland.[129]

According to Amen-Ra and the Empress, the Mound builders were given this side of our planet as a promised land for honoring the mother, while women were increasingly victimized back home in the east.

"Our society is based on the woman envisioning the Law and the man enforcing it," the Empress recalled her grandmother teaching her. "In our world the woman inherits the land, not the man." Her words reminded me of an interview I had some years ago with Ernie Longwalker, an advocate for Indigenous nations here. He said the drum in Indian culture represents the heartbeat of the women, and initiation into manhood includes helping teenages to understand the pains women endure in life.

The Empress said before the white man came, men did not rule over women but worked together. "The woman was viewed as precious and she was respected," she said, recalling her grandmother's words. Black women are not the only leaders advancing this idea.

[Seth Muhammad, a member of the Washitaw and the Nation of Islam. Louisiana, 2000. Photo credit: Lamont Muhammad]

Dr. Malachi Z. York, a.k.a. Amunnubi Raa, leader of the United Nuwaubian Nation of the Moors, would also agree with the African origins of American culture. He leads a community that is based in Georgia, where they have erected replicas of Ancient Egypt on close to 500 acres. Dr. Raa teaches that the name Nuwaubian is derived from the word Nuwba (Nuba), in Southern Sudan, which he said would include Ethiopia, Uganda and Kenya. The root word for Nuwaubians, Nubians and Nabi is Nub or Nuwb, meaning "color inclining to Black... kinky or woolly haired people." In his book: *Let's Set The Record Straight,* he described the Olmec civilization as "the original woolly haired, dark-olive toned people" who originally came to the Americas from Nuwba of South and Central Africa long before the Christian era. He almost completely rejects the slave ship notion.

> *... Let's humor this notion for one moment. Human beings were packed on the bottom of a ship, to sail across the ocean, a trip that takes at least three months, right (?) Now these humans eat, right (?) How else would you keep them alive(?) After they eat, they urinate and pass feces. How did they survive? You are talking about 15 pounds of feces a day, not to mention urine. They would have drowned. So eliminate the slave ship story, it's very illogical.* [130]

The Nuwaubians also teach their people in the Americas to stop referring to themselves as former slaves because slavery was a legal institution in America but kidnapping and torture is unlawful. These and other arguments form the base for many of the land wars raging in US and world courts for tribal recognitions and sovereignty rights within former colonial borders. The classifications can transform a tribal group from poverty stricken to filthy rich.

According to Qualla Kuthera Howard, a Black (Indian) woman born on the Qualla Reservation in North Carolina, the US government is fighting hard to dissuade groups from reclaiming their sovereignty status and land. In a brief telephone interview from Schenectady, New York, she said only 150 of the 350 Indigenous tribes in North America are officially recognized. Only the Navajo and the Iroquois enjoy sovereignty status. In New York State, she continued,

---
[130] Dr. Malachi Z. York, *Let's Set The Record Straight*, p. 178

the Oneida Tribe signed a 100-year land lease with the US government that has expired. They are in court because "the Oneida want their land back," she said.

The Empress said she includes in her family the Olmec, Maya, Aztec, Garifuna, Arawak, Carib, Taino and many other nations of the Americas. In 1993, she said, her group received Indigenous status by a UN non-governmental organization. The Empress has addressed the U.N. world body as the official representative of the Washitaw. Her claim to the land is based on what she called flaws in the implementation of the infamous Louisiana Purchase. She said the illegal land transfer violated bilateral treaties and international law when her 86, 883 acres were included in the transfer.

Beyond those arguments, she and many other voices are making a case for the fact that the entire US sits on lands stolen mostly from a dark skinned people. "We should not be limited to Africa and the east. Our footprints are throughout our earth and we can not allow others to box us up and rip us off our lands forever," she demanded.

APPENDIX B

The Indigenous of the World Complain to the UN
By Lamont Muhammad
08.14.01

UNITED NATIONS - Maria Callejas Salinas and Patricia Pena traveled eight days in a bus from the Costa Chica in Mexico to join an estimated 400 to 600 other representatives of native people here for the Seventh International Day of the World's Indigenous People, August 9 and 10.

At the end, unfortunately, one participant described the meetings as more of an opportunity for the wealthy to study the poor than to consult with them for informed policies that might relieve suffering.

"I've been to enough meetings for the sake of talking," Ms. Pena told *The Final Call* through an interpreter. "My friend Maria (an African Mexican) came to speak to the issue of compensation for the Africans who were enslaved in Mexico and continue to be discriminated against there. I came to represent the cause of the indigenous and to demand that Africans in Mexico be included in the political process with us…

"It was nice to learn we are not alone. And we are pleased with the contacts we have made with other participants here but we came seeking practical solutions to problems facing our people. Not to talk," she said.

[The Costa Chica is on the southwestern corner of Mexico, where large populations of original inhabitants live.]

According to Ellen McGuffie, an U.N. information official, indigenous issues reached the floor of the General Assembly (GA) in the 1970s. The UN High Commissioner for Human Rights, other subcommittees and non-government organizations kicked off the International Decade of the World's Indigenous People (1995 to 2004). The International Day began here in 1994 and will run through the decade. The purpose, officials say, "is to strengthen international cooperation for the solution of problems faced by indigenous people in such areas as human rights, the environment, development, education and health," an official press release said. Next year will mark the establishment of a Permanent Forum for the discussion of indigenous issues here, officials announced.

Critics called the sessions symbol without substance and described the pomp and ceremony as a way for the wealthy to claim they give a hearing to the wailing and moaning of those in the shrinking natural margins of the booming global economy.

Participants complained about the vanishing forests they worship, the increasingly polluted waters (from industrialization) they fish from and drink, and of forms of cultural imperialism they say is being imposed on their traditional lifestyles.

"The bad news," a UN official said to a group in the basement of the Secretariat Building on the last day, is that there are fewer resources (International Monetary Fund, World Bank and other UN Agency funds) to divide between you this year.

"The good news is that everybody knows you already know how to work with nothing," the UN Environment Program representative said. He was flanked by other UN agency representatives at the head of an oval of tables in a conference room, filled with a variety of people draped in colorful expressions of culture and aesthetics that were slightly spoiled by a sense of disappointment on some of their colorful faces.

"We are living under the law of the Taghut (misguided men) but communication is important," said Sher Malik of the Indigenous Peoples Survival Foundation. Listening can sometimes bring about a commitment to change without violence, he said. But a Nobel Peace Laureate refused to attend.

"The reason for my absence is that the UN system and those countries that play a hegemonic role at the UN continue to address the subject of indigenous peoples without the due respect that we deserve, and to question our identity and rights," Rigoberta Menchu Tum, "UNESCO's Ambassador for a Culture of Peace," wrote in a special statement that was distributed at the conference.

"In the recent appointment of the UN Special Reporteur for the study of violations of human rights and fundamental freedoms of indigenous peoples, the old paternalism prevailed, insisting in treating us as inferior persons, subjects of study, and not recognizing us as actors who can define and determine our own destiny," she wrote. Others on the ground agree.

"Most indigenous people do not attend UN meetings," said an organizer for the Ohatchee Cherokee Tribe in New York who chose not to attend. "How can you have a meeting for "The World's" indigenous people with no Africans? We stopped attending years ago. The whole thing is a joke designed to prop up the Uncle Tom members of indigenous groups who benefit by selling their people down the drain," said Linda Daniels.

This writer did see four continental Africans in the sessions.

"For these devils, calling the indigenous to a meeting is a chance for them to take pictures of the natives smoking peace pipes and to buy art. That's all it is," said Farrell X of the Cree Nation. "I once worked for the Bureau of Indian Affairs in Washington D.C. They didn't help any Indians. All they did was store millions in art in the attic of the South Building of the Department of Interior. These meetings are rubber stamps to cover devilishment," he suggested, offering some advise.

"My message to the righteous among the indigenous is to hold on. These greedy people are killing themselves more than they are affecting us. The land will soon be back in our hands by the promise and power of the Most High Creator, not the UN," he concluded.

APPENDIX C

Black Mexico Is Spreading Wings
By Lamont Muhammad
08.27.01

[Patricia Pena (seated) and Maria C. Salinas displayed their wares at United African Movement meeting, Harlem, 200. Photo credit: Lamont Muhammad.]

The record of the Africans who traded and settled among the ancient cultures of Mexico before the Spanish conquest and subsequent slave era is one of the best-kept secrets of the age. Millions of Africans in Mexico do not exist by government decree. The same applies to the indigenous populations there, advocates complain. They charge the children of the invader/settler with practicing forms of neglecting and ignoring original people and cultures into extinction.

Two women endured an eight-day bus trip from the shrinking margins of rural southern Mexico to represent the burning issues that face the African and Chatino people on the world stage of the United Nations (UN) in New York and to start a movement for change.

"Brothers and Sisters, please receive a strong affection from my Black community in Oaxaca (pronounced: Wa-ha-ka), Mexico," Maria Callejas Salinas said in words that were translated from her Spanish for an English speaking radio audience in New York August 8. She and Patricia Pena came to join some 500 other representatives of native people for the International Day of the World's Indigenous People at the UN August 9 and 10.

Ms. Salinas said she was thankful to indigenous groups for making it possible for her to travel to New York to tell her story. But she bashed the ruling society in Mexico as a bastion of white supremacy that systematically ignores Africans "simply because we are Black." Her traveling companion, agreed.

"We all have suffered the same oppression from the bearded one (white man). But we recognize that an even bigger crime was committed against the Blacks. (The white man) stole their language and history," Ms. Pena, a member of the Chatino nation said.

The ironic twist to this story is that dark people in Mexico were responsible for most of what the country celebrates as ancient culture. According to Professor Edward Bynum of the University of Massachusetts, Africans established or at least heavily influenced the first high culture in Mexico centuries before the arrival of the Spanish.

"The (Mexican) Olmec kings, like the (Egyptian) pharaohs, wore a duel crown... Both had the royal flail; the plumed serpent suddenly replaces the royal jaguar; purple is the royal color. The Olmec books, most of which were burned by Europeans, had black and red kings in royal purple," he wrote in *The African Unconscious*...

Interestingly, most Africans who live in Mexico today live where the Olmecs settled. The great "Negroid colossi," as Professor Ivan Van Sertima described, were found along Mexico's Gulf Coast in Veracruz. They established mission outposts, experts say, where Salinas and Pena call home. The Costa Chica is a 200-mile long Pacific coastal region that begins just southeast of Acapulco, Guerrero and ends in Puerto Angel, Oaxaca. There are an estimated 24 African Mexican villages in the region, organizers report. Archeologists continue to unearth Olmec artifacts there.

"I have seen workers remove sticks with lights on them and a material they could not penetrate," Pena recalled. She told this writer she and her people know of underground caves with floors and doors. "There had to be another people here before my people. We don't make floors and doors," she explained.

The late University of Veracruz Professor Gonzalo Aquirre Beltran argued in his book *The Black Population of Mexico,* that there were 250,000 Africans in the Costa Chica region before the first Spanish slave ship arrived. Mexican history is layered in African heroics and contradictions. Blacks were with Cortez when he defeated the Aztecs. But Africans have consistently fought side by side with the indigenous to resist oppression, as Pena said, and in one special case, the two bloods produced "the George Washington of the Mexican Revolution (1819 -1821)" as well as other heroes of the Revolution of 1910. Vincente Guerrero, a former slave, defeated the Spanish forces, negotiated an end to slavery in Mexico and eventually rose to be president of the Republic against great opposition. The rich wanted independence from Spain but wanted to maintain the institution of white supremacy in Mexico. Unfortunately, when Guerrero negotiated the Independence Plan of Iguala in 1821, he and his people had inadvertently agreed to no preferential treatment for victims of colonization. The Faustian Pact made it illegal for a member of Congress to mention the race of individuals on the chamber floor. It also prohibited government and church records from identifying people by race, according to Ted Vincent, *The Daily Challenge,* "Afro-Mexicans Who Fused a National Identity." When President Guerrero began to construct schools and libraries in the Costa Chica he was run back into the mountains from which he had once waged revolution, according to Joel A. Rogers, author of *Worlds Great Men of Color, Vol. II*] Guerrero was captured and executed after a mock trial, Mr. Rogers wrote. When news spread of Guerrero's murder riots and other forms of protest rocked Mexico until some conspirators paid with their lives and others were driven from the country. But the fix was in.

This researcher discovered the treachery Spain heaped on Black people early in the research. For nearly 800 years the Moors raised Spain, which in turn raised Europe out of the "Dark Ages." Moors taught the Spanish to read, to eat properly, to pave their roads, to light the streets of their cities and to irrigate their lands. When Spain expelled the Moors in 1492, Spain became a major African slave-trading nation and the first nation to enact a public policy of enforced illiteracy for Blacks in 1517, according to Claud Anderson, author of *Dirty Little Secrets*.

At least the secret is out, judging from Salinas and Pena. They told this writer they were pleased with the contacts they made while here and looked forward to networking with progressive forces in this country in a drive for mutual uplift.

APPENDIX D

Nzingha, Warrior Queen of Nature?
By Lamont Ra Muur Muhammad
10.19.01

AMERICAN BEACH, Florida - Anta Majigeen Njaay, a beautiful tall and shiny Black Wolof girl, as admirers described her, was 13 years old when Zephaniah Kingsley, Jr., a maritime merchant, planter, and slave owner from Spanish East Florida, bought her in Havana in 1806.

Before her 14th birthday the planter openly declared her his wife, she managed his significantly large plantation household not far from here, and was pregnant with child.

By age 19, Anna Jai Kingsley, as she came to be known, had achieved freedom for herself and three children, owned her own plantation and had earned a respectful reputation that continues to be documented and celebrated.

Her great-great-great-great granddaughter participated in the Fourth Annual Kingsley Heritage Celebration on Fort George Island near here October 14, 2001.

But MaVynee Betsch, 66, is not an accumulator of property, slaves and wealth like her famous ancestor. In fact, The "Beach Lady," as she is affectionately and mockingly known, said she prefers to live "like a hermit crab on the beach." Her mission is to challenge a glitzy materialism she said is "robbing the earth of her raiment and leaving Mother Nature exposed.

She explained that she invested her "considerable inheritance" in saving whales, butterflies and other environmental efforts. "I sponsored a conference in Brazil," she said, holding erect her elegant six-foot long frame. She talked in expressively vivid pictures.

"These people dam rivers. That is like putting a chastity belt on the earth.

"Backward idiots depend on machines. Wise people depend on mind," she said. She, in the spirit of the ancients, complains that men, especially white men, have too much influence on world affairs. Her subject that day at the 203rd anniversary of the birth of the Kingsley Plantation, which was sponsored by the U.S. National Park Service, was "Nzingha: Amazon Queen of Matamba West Africa."

"Look at the curve of my hair," she told the 100 or so on-lookers that gathered under a white tent on that hot and humid day. "Doesn't it look like West Africa?" Her-7 foot mane loops off of her head like "a fat seven," she likes to say. She drapes it over her forearm like a shawl to keep it off the ground.

"Look at Florida. Is it a seven? Is Africa a fat seven? Look at Brazil – a seven! That's what I'm about, like Nzingha," whom she said her grandfather admired and often discussed. Ms. MaVynne is a graduate of Oberlin College, a former operatic performer on American and European stages, is the older sister to former Spelman College president Johnetta Coles and the granddaughter of Florida's first Black millionaire Abraham Lincoln Lewis.

[MaVynne Betsch, 2001. Photo credit: Linda Fletcher]

Before her presentation on the plantation, she sat in a broken blue plastic chair across the small road from a trailer she uses for a home and museum. On one side 60-foot sand dunes are darted with palmetto palms, opposite a row of boarded wooden ruins that she said once featured the likes of Duke Ellington and Count

Basie. Behind the ruins were sand and sea. Otherwise, her eyes patrolled the rest of the 12 streets her grandfather named on the original 200-acre beachfront paradise he bought here the year she was born.

Mr. Lewis acquired American Beach in 1935 for the enjoyment of his family and those in his employ who were thrifty and wise enough to save and buy a piece of this Jacksonville island paradise. He was one of seven founders of the Afro-American Life Insurance Company.

MaVynne recalled to Linda Fletcher her memories of her grandfather standing in the southeasterly breeze and calling for Queen Nzingha. "He used to say 'she's coming.'" And so she is here, in the Beach Lady's determination to defeat a steady encroachment of golf courses, marinas and beachfront Condos on her piece of history.

According to MaVynne, the Queen of Angola sought refuge and direction in nature. She achieved victories over internal enemies, the Portuguese, the Pope and even inspired rebellion in Brazil with the elite Palmares, MaVynne argues, came from Angola.

"Did you know that Nzingha lived off honey supplied by a Queen Bee?" She asked.

"This 'male is God' concept is barely 4000-years-old. We have been on this planet in a matriarchal culture much longer…

"Look at what you are denying your brain. All that is still in the back of your little spine waiting to give you your power again," she charged the guilty.

She said she believes women, like mother earth herself, must be consulted before men can propose changes. She said she sees her work in those terms in order to change the world back for the better.

APPENDIX E

Sembene Pictures the Voice of the Ancients
By Lamont Muhammad
05.09.01

HARLEM, New York – Who in the world gave birth to the "father of African film," Ousmane Sembene?

Does the apparent love, appreciation and sometimes awe for the feminine principle that comes across in his work come from the security he experienced in the womb of his mother – when she travailed to bare and protect him, even in the face of 1923 colonial Africa?

Or, was he nurtured by an extended maternal culture that formed the near 80-year-old film maker into the critical defender of women and advocate for returning women to their rightful thrown of influence?

"I am just an artist," explained Mr. Sembene to a packed house of film students and admirers at the final session of the 7th Annual African Film Festival New York (AFFNY) April 29. "I don't have the solutions," he told the audience at the Arturo Schomburg Center for Research in Black Culture that afternoon. "(I design) my work to raise questions," he said.

His latest film, *Faat – Kine* (2000), included in the AFFNY, tells the story of a single mother's successful business, her aspiring children, her two ex-husbands and other changing roles some women are adapting to in modern Africa.

In Africa's first feature length film, *Black Girl* (1966), Sembene told the true story of a young Senegalese woman who sought a way out of poverty in Dakar. When she later discovered a greater exploitation and helpless confinement in France, she committed suicide.

His other works, censored and banned at home at times in Senegal, cut on all sides of politics and religion in Africa. His films are known to raise questions about the effect Islam, Christianity and traditional African religions have had and continue to have on African people, as well as the corruption that pervades African politics and governance.

"I am not against religion but I know Islamic leaders who are thieves. I know false priests… The traditional religions are great but they do not prevent disease and hunger," he explained, describing Africans as a trusting people who "change religions like other people change shirts.

"I just don't want worship to get in the way of development in Africa," he told the attentive audience against a two-rhythm response. His French presentation was followed by an English translation by Professor Samba Gadjigo of Mt Holyoke College.

[Women at work in Nima, Ghana, 1996, by Lamont Muhammad.]

Sembene films raise questions about government officials and village elders who rule by a consensus that does not include women. Nevertheless, women are at the center of much of the problem solving in his films.

Sembene is not from the elite/ancient high casts of Africa. He was a fisherman as a young boy among the Diola people of the Casamance region in Senegal, according to *Third World Film Making and the West*, by Roy Armes. Expelled from school as a teenager, he worked as a mechanic, then bricklayer before he joined the French Army at 19. After four years of service in France and Africa, he returned to Africa to work in Dakar and got involved with a railway strike. Later, he went back to France and joined the Communist Party. The 10 years he worked on the docks of Marseilles gave him the material he needed for his first novel, *Le docker noir* (1956). According to his book, it helped Sembene realize he would never properly serve his people in the language of their former colonizer. He studied filmmaking on scholarship in Moscow between 1961 and 1962 and is arguably the first cinematographer to shoot movies in color in Africa and the first to shoot them in languages indigenous to the continent. His other films include: *Borom Sarret* (1964), *The Money Order* (1968), *Tauw* (1969), *Emitai* (God of Thunder, 1971), *Xala* (the Curse, 1974), *Ceddo* (the common people, 1977), *Camp De Thiaroye* (1987) and *Guelwaar* (the noble one, 1993).

A theme Sembene often repeated during the question and answer period was that Africans must accept responsibility for deciding the solutions for her many problems.

"There are four colonial systems that have divided our dreams to unite the continent beyond colonial (imposed) boundaries. (Today our progress is delayed) by wars, disease (and other man-made) calamities" he said. He emphasized that answers "must not be expected" to come from the United States or Europe, especially on the issue of female incision, he and others argued. The procedure is practiced in 37 of the 56 states that comprise the Organization of African Unity, Sembene said.

"Yes it is wrong," an attractive young woman cried in French, translated by Prof. Gadjigo. She confessed in the Q&A line that she too had felt the sting of the knife at home in Africa. But she agreed with Sembene's caution.

"I am concerned that all of these other people who have never experienced the culture stay out of the discussion."

When pressed to reveal the secret to his success, Sembene, whose sense of humor and insights kept most people on the edge of their seats in the Langston Hughes Auditorium said: "You can be a splash on the front page for two weeks (and die out). Or you can love your people, stay in the background (and raise questions that make them think)."

APPENDIX F

The Gullah and Sierra Leone
By Lamont Muhammad
10.26.01

SEA ISLANDS, Florida - Uncle Ben, the Carolina Rice box icon, was probably a Geechee or Gullah, a direct descendant of the Rice Coast Africans, especially from Sierra Leone, who made Charlestown, now Charleston, one of the wealthiest communities in the North American colonies.

Gullah country begins in these islands off from Jacksonville and runsup and along the moist, semitropical and swampy coastline of Georgia and South Carolina. By the early 1700s slave traders knew Africans from the Gambia and Sierra Leone commanded high prices from here to Charlestown, where the land was perfect for rice cultivation.

"When slave traders arrived in Charlestown with slaves from the rice growing region, they were careful to advertise their origin on auction posters or in newspaper announcements, sometimes noting that the slaves were 'accustomed to the planting of rice.' Traders, who arrived in Charlestown with slaves from other parts of Africa where rice was not traditionally grown, such as Nigeria, often found that their slaves fetched lower prices. In some cases, they could sell no slaves at all and had to sail away to another port.

[Joseph A. Opala, *The Gullah: Rice, Slavery, and the Sierra Leone-American Connection*]

These Africans from the "Rice Coast" or the "Windward Coast," were forced into a new physical environment they already understood, tobare the insulting burden of slavery along side folks they already knew. These skilled Africans gave rise to something rare – Africans who have maintained their Africaness in the U.S., against all odds. More than Black Americans as a whole, Gullahs use African names, continue to tell African folk tales, and carry on ancient African traditions, such as basket weaving and carvings, and enjoy a rich cuisine based primarily on rice. They also speak a language that is arguably more complex than Standard English because "Creole," the so-called "broken English," is actually enriched with African words and sounds. It is similar to Sierra Leone Krio.

[Mr. Opapla was commissioned by the U.S. Information Service, Freetown, Sierra Leone, the first town in Africa established by returning Gullahs in 1788, according to Llaila O. Africa, author of *The Gullah.*]

The Kingsley Plantation on Fort George Island here is at the southern end of the Sea Islands. The National Park Service (NPS) today uses the plantation as a model of systems that made an efficient, profitable plantation – by way of the knowledge Africans brought to the Western Hemisphere. This plantation produced Sea Island cotton, indigo, citrus, sugar cane and corn.

Zephaniah Kingsley, Jr., a slave trader and planter, bought this plantation in 1814, when the eastern coast of the United States stopped at Georgia and Spain needed mercenaries, sometimes free and sometimes runaway Gullah, to protect East Florida and Spain's export bound bootie-laden ships. He was born in Bristol, England in 1765 but he was reared in a Charlestown, South Carolina Quaker household. It was probably in that predominately African community that Mr. Kingsley learned about business, agriculture and how to manipulate the labor of skilled free and enslaved Africans.

Kingsley purchased this plantation two years after the Gullah and Seminole nations had defeated the U.S. Marines in Spanish Florida in 1812. The Spanish hired the Gullah and Seminoles to protect their valuables from pirates. Planters like Kingsley in Spanish East Florida, were encouraged to "manumit their slaves and incorporate them into a three-caste society of whites, free people of color, and slaves. Kingsley openly declared an African his wife and she ran his house.

That level of freedom for Africans proved to be a problem for southern slave holders in the U.S. who consistently complained to the government that East Florida was a haven for runaways.

Things began to change, however, when Spain was forced to let go claims here in 1821, East Florida became a new U.S. territory, a whites started moving into Florida in record numbers. The new residents viewed all black people – slave and free alike – as members of an inferior race and unworthy of freedom. The new society would be composed of two castes only; there would be free whites and enslaved blacks, with no place for free blacks," a piece by Daniel L. Schafer on Anna Kingsley said. What had amounted to skirmishes between the U.S. and Spain in Florida up until 1821, became all out wars between the U.S. government and people of color. The U.S. was determined to eliminate independent Gullah and Seminole bands in Florida, lower Alabama, Louisiana and Texas, history shows.

Denmark Vessey led the first major Gullah revolt in the U.S. in 1822 with "Gullah Jack" of Angola leading the charge. By 1834 a law was passed here that made it illegal to educate free Blacks and slaves. Whites feared that educated Blacks, in the wake of the Denmark Vessey and Nat Turner revolts, "would seek justice through any means," Afrika said.

In "The Negro War" of 1842 the U.S. declared war on the independent communities of the Gullah and Seminoles and marched the survivors to Oklahoma at gunpoint. Others had distinguished themselves so well against U.S. troops that they were hired by Mexico to patrol that border. Later, some of the Buffalo Soldiers were hired to protect the white settlers in the west from indigenous people trying to protect their land. The history is full of contradictions.

In 1858 Harriet Tubman establishes the first Black American hospital for the Underground Railroad in the Sea Islands.

At the same time, the first soldiers to strike in the U.S. Army were Gullahs refusing to accept pay until paid at the same rate as white Union soldiers in 1863. The strike lasted 18 months.

By 1865, General William T. Sherman issued Field Order #15, designating the Sea Islands and 30 miles inland from Charleston, Gullah owned country. White folks had abandoned the islands on "Gun Shoot Day," when the Union defeated the Confederate Army in 1861, according to Afrika. President Andrew Johnson changed the order four months later and Black people have been striving and struggling to maintain land as an independent people here ever since, many complain.

According to Dr. Jack Felder, a Gullah biochemist, Seminoles (Semi – noles), were the children of the Africans and those who white folks called Indians. He said the children of women raped by white man were thrown in the river. "That's how we stayed Black," he said.

APPENDIX G

Slavery and Florida Revisited
By Lamont Muhammad
11.22.01

FORT GEORGE ISLAND, Florida – Zephaniah Kingsley, Jr. purchased this lush island off today's Jacksonville, in 1814, a period the English refer to as the Elizabethan era. Slavery was legal in the U.S., at the time, but the importation of African slaves was illegal.

Here, in East Florida, under a Spanish coat of arms, as it was at the time, Mr. Kingsley could import and export slaves and agricultural products anywhere in the world at will.

Palm trees lined the broad avenues that divided the precious fields of Sea Island cotton, corn, indigo and sugar cane. The slave master and his family lived in a white colonial styled mini-mansion. His slaves lived in a fifth of a mile down the main road in the center of the plantation in a 32-tabby cement cabin semi-circle.

Today, this historic preserve is used by the U.S. National ParkService (N.P.S.) as a stage for discussions and reenactments of events here that shaped the course of modern history. Slaves who labored here, for example, went on to themselves own slaves, cultivate, toil and trade. A few slaves, along with

Kingsley, eventually migrated to a newly independent Haiti. They moved to escape East Florida after it became apart of the U.S., an N.P.S. brochure said.

At Kingsley Heritage Celebration 2001, October 13 and 14, the N.P.S. sponsored lectures, demonstrations, book signings, traditional storytelling and featured a presentation by a descendent of Mr. Kingsley and the former African slave he freed and married by the time they moved here 203-years ago. This seemingly unconventional action on the part of Kingsley was possible under the Spanish flag, within its three-caste society of whites, free people of color, and slaves. In the encroaching U.S. there were "free whites and enslaved blacks, with no place for free blacks," a presenter here explained.

"Blacks and Seminoles kept the British and Americans out of Spanish territory" and protected her bootie-laden ships bound for export, explained N.P.S. Ranger, Ralph Smith, a Black Seminole, draped in full Seminole regalia. He told listeners here the Seminoles defeated the U.S. Marines in 1812 in Spanish Florida.

"But in 1821 Florida became a part of U.S. territory and the plantation owners in Georgia, Mississippi, Alabama and the Carolinas petitioned the U.S. government stating that Florida was a haven for runaways and they wanted to do something about it. The Indian Removal Act had already been imposed elsewhere. When it came to Florida it had a new twist. All Native Americans would be pushed out to Arkansas, now known as Oklahoma and all Black people would go back into slavery. We fought for seven years," Ranger Smith said.

In 1828 Kingsley authored - *A Treatise on the Patriarchal, or Co-operative System of Society As It Exists in Some Governments...Under the Name Slavery.* It expressed his opposition to the new oppressive laws the U.S. was imposing on free and enslaved Blacks in Florida. "Power may for a while triumph over weakness and misfortune. But as all nature (from the eternal principle of self) takes part with weakness against power, the re-action finally must be terrible and overwhelming," he wrote, suggesting "power" ruled without justice will ultimately lose.

Other whites, recognizing the fact they were completely outnumbered by Blacks, feared educating them, believing literate Blacks posed the greatest danger.

In 1837 Kingsley fled Florida and established a colony for his family and some of his former slaves in Haiti, the N.P.S. brochure said.

By 1842 the U.S. government had declared war on all dark people who refused to submit here in Florida, lower Alabama, Louisiana and Texas. In "The Negro War," as it was called, this government massacred men, women and children and marched survivors to Oklahoma at gunpoint. Later the script flipped when the Union required the assistance of Black people in order to defeat the Confederacy.

A surviving Civil War structure associated with Black Union Army troops still stands across the St. Johns River here at Dames Point. A member of the 54th Massachusetts Volunteer Infantry Re-Enactors Company "I" of Glory fame, said they were "the first Blacks to fight in the Civil War." Two sons of Fredrick Douglas and one of Sojourner Truth were among the "88 percent learned men" who comprised the celebrated unit, Chaplin Clifford Pierce explained. There were a total of 170 U.S. Colored Troop Units, with as many as 200,000 Black soldiers during the Civil War, records show. The "Colored Troops" controlled ship access along the river, officials said.

Baba Ishangi of Brooklyn, New York, attended the event. He was invited to Jacksonville to work on a "Living African History Exhibit" and was subsequently invited to the event here to read, but was not impressed with what he described as N.P.S. spins on history.

"I'm a descendent of a great African people. I haven't seen any of them here yet. Everybody they mention here married somebody white or was given this or given that. The man (Black Seminole) told me the Seminole had Irish in 'em. If I listen any longer I'm gonna go get a flag and run down the road chanting 'thank God for slavery.'" He left to get something to eat. Later, Mr. Ishangi, Kala JoJo and Queen Nur, nationally renowned storytellers, kicked the African traditions for two audiences. They were followed on the final day by MaVynee Betsch, the stately Kingsley descendent who came to talk about "Nzingha: Amazon Queen of Matamba West Africa."

Head slave quarters on Kingsley Plantation, Florida;

(l) Ranger Ralph Smith sports the regalia of his ancestors, the Black Seminoles at the Kingsley Plantation, Florida, 2001; (r) Dr. Jack Felder on 125th Street in Harlem, 2001

Members of the 54th Massachusetts volunteer Infantry Re-enactors Company; - Ruins of tabby cement slave cabins on Kingsley Plantation, 2001; 6- A view from the beach of black area on American Beach, Amelia Island, Florida;

Black Mexico: The Greatest Story Never Told

American Beach Black History Museum, 2001; 8- Factories stain the sky near Jacksonville, Florida, 2001; 9- Linda Fletcher (right), interviews Kitty Wilson Evans of the Historical Center of York County, South Carolina, 2001; Photos by Lamont Muhammad.

APPENDIX H

Education for Black New Yorkers?
By Lamont Muhammad
08.30.03

HARLEM – In May 1993, Robert Jackson, city councilman, and angry parent, became the lead plaintiff in a suit filed by a coalition of advocacy groups here, that accused the state of cheating city public school students out of billions of dollars and thereby cheating and denying mostly Black and Latino students a decent education.

In January 2001, Manhattan Supreme Court Justice Leland DeGrasse, agreed and ordered the state to make the proper financial adjustments to improve the city high schools, in particular.

In June 2002, a state appeals court ruled that Justice DeGrasse had gone "too far" with his ruling. The Appellate Division's 4 to 1 ruling supported New York Governor, George Pataki's argument instead that the state is only required to provide a "minimally adequate educational opportunity" to children in this city – up to the eighth grade.

Governor Pataki appointed four out of the five Appeals Court judges.

Mr. Jackson and company vowed to continue the fight.

Then in June 2003, the highest court in the state ruled against Pataki and in favor of Jackson's people.

"After a century of fighting for our children's fair share of state education funding, the Court of Appeals has acknowledged that the children of New York City, 80 percent of whom are Black and brown, deserve the funding necessary for a meaningful high school education," a jubilant Denise Morgan declared to reporters after the decision. The expert on race and public schools litigated the case from the beginning.

"We have been experiencing this type of seesaw since we have been in this country with white folks, said Sharonne Salaam, executive director of People United for Children. "You get one victory that you think is a victory. Then somebody else tells you it is not a victory. Then you are fighting to get the victory back and so forth and so on," she said during an exclusive interview at her office here.

"What we are talking about is racism and white folks desire to protect their own future. The real problem," she said, is that "when these problems pop up, we turn around and seek remedies, support and guidance from the people who plot against us - and, we expect to get justice. If something is wrong with our children, we go to them. If something is wrong with our schools, we go to them." That is why we are on a slippery slope and things for us will only get worst until we learn to do for ourselves that which we require of others, she argued.

The public school system in this city is the largest in the country. Battles have waged here historically between parents and teachers unions, between teachers unions and administrators, between school administrators and the city, between the city and the state and between the state and federal government. The victims, of course, have been the children. As Ms. Salaam pointed out, "our children are going to school with no books, they are over-crammed up in classrooms, and some are studying in hallways... Something needs to be done. The government says they are only required to educate to the 8th grade. What do we say? What is our plan? White folks have plans."

She cited federal policies of imposing standardized testing that tie the hands of teachers in the public schools who now have to prepare students to pass tests as opposed to teach them to think. In addition, some 3,000 teachers were fired this year because they failed to pass the certification exams critics argue are culturally biased.

"We cannot blame the white man for doing what he does best to protect his own people. We must figure out whom we are going to protect. Are we going to protect our people or are we going to sit back and allow them to be run over by someone who wants to protect his?" Then, Ms. Salaam recalled her own experience.

"I can remember - I do not remember how many days we went - but we had a one room shack where we learned that survival skills were not taught in school. We had interaction between the community and the child and the interaction built in a commitment for the survival of that particular child. We don't have that anymore and we cannot expect our children to be educated to throw others out of their jobs."

Finally, she said, we must develop confidence to build institutions that educate our teachers to educate our children and stop attempting to prove to others that we are human beings who are worthy of their help. "We are in need of a healing in Africa and throughout the African Diaspora, that we might recognize as a people, our need to connect globally and support our common interests as a people. Today, we talk a good game with phrases like 'leave no child behind. We can't leave them behind because we are walking over top each one of them making it up the latter," she concluded.

APPENDIX I

The Toll Paid by Those Who Forge a Way
By Lamont Muhammad
08.03.03

HARLEM - George Grandville Monah James, professor of theology, math, Greek, Latin, logic, philosophy and social science, published his seminal book *Stolen Legacy*, in 1954. The book exposed the fact that what had been celebrated as Greek contributions toscience and culture were in fact authored by Black Egyptians long before. The distinguished author "died under mysterious circumstances shortly after publication," Anthony Browder wrote in his *Nile Valley Contributions to Civilization.*

Dr. Chiekh Anta Diop, author of *African Origins of Civilization: Reality of Myth? The Cultural Unity of Black Africa, Precolonial Black Africa* and *Civilization or Barbarism,* suddenly died in his sleep at 62. It happened when he decided to get involved in politics, recalled the translator of Dr. Diop's *Civilization or Barbarism,* Professor Yaa-Lengi M. Ngemi, director of The African Research and Educational Institute, Inc., here. "No autopsy was conducted. He was buried quickly and many suspected foul play," the author of *Murder in the Congo-Zaire* told *The Final Call* in a recent interview.

Dr. Amos N. Wilson, author of *The Developmental Psychology of the Black Child, Awakening the Natural Genius of Black Children, The Falsification of the Afrikan Consciousness* and *Black Power*, was a relatively young Afrikan scholar who is no longer with us. Many questions abound within segments of the Black community here.

These are but three examples of what many argue are tolls those who forge against the tide of established scholarship must pay on the upward drive to reveal the true history of man and mankind. But the focus of this discussion is what becomes of the others who live. In the final chapters of the lives of these pioneers who manage to avoid the death and other traps, who survive the physical and financial tolls from traveling to research true history, few get the credit and security they deserve in their declining years, observers told *The Final Call*.

Dr. Yosef Ben-Jochannon, authored *African Origins of the Major Western Religions, Black Man of the Nile, A Chronology of the Bible, Abu Simbel to Ghizeh, Africa: Mother of Western Civilization* and *We The Black Jews*. Dr. Ben, as he is known, taught at Pace and Cornell Universities in New York, is a Senior Lecturer at Al Azhar University in Cairo, Egypt, and is credited with taking 30,000 Africans born in the west back to Egypt.

"Dr. Ben is 88 years old," said Ego Hayes, a towering Black retired school principle here who travels with his wife and researchers like Runoko Rashidi, an expert on African foundations of contemporary civilization. Mr. Hayes, who lectures himself, said he often donates the honorariums he receives to Dr. Ben. He explained that "most Black college professors, like Dr. Ben, work as adjunct professors. That means they are not on the tenure track. They can work for 50 years and not have retirement," he lamented, citing another example.

[Professor Ivan Van Sertima (center) in Belize, 2000. Photo credit: Lamont Muhammad]

Professor Ivan Van Sertima authored *They Came Before Columbus: The African Presence in Ancient America*. He is editor and founder of the *Journal of African Civilizations,* was appointed by UNESCO to the *International Commission for Rewriting the Scientific and Cultural History of Mankind* and appeared before the U.S. Congress to challenge the "Christopher Columbus discovered America" myth. He was an Associate Professor at Rutgers University and a Visiting Professor at Princeton. "Van Sertima receives no pension," Mr. Hayes revealed during a recent interview here at his home.

"Understanding your own history will get you off the tenure track and get you fired at most major universities. White folks are not going to finance the enemy (truth). When you consider the fact that the U.S. withheld its dues to the U.N. because UNESCO was trying to get the world out of the Euro-centric view of history," you will realize how serious some people are at preserving falsehood. The Congress just voted this pass year to restore the money to the U.N. "if they do not revisit the subject of trying to change history," he said. Hayes was referring to a colloquium UNESCO did on the subject of the ethnocentricity of the Egyptians at the U.N. in the 1970s. There were a number of European scholars arguing the Euro-centric view and there were two Africans, Dr. Chiekh Anta Diop and his foremost student, Theophile Obinga, Hayes recalled.

"At the end of the conference, UN officials suggested that everybody employ the painstaking methods Diop and Obinga used because they were the only presenters that brought proof. White folks used their opinions of what history should be," he said.

Sekou Books, as he prefers to be identified, is a well respected 125th Street bookseller and lecturer in his own right. He said white supremacy is based on a lie that was created in the 1770s as a justification for slavery. "The only problem with the myth or lie is that these Europeans have never come up with an alphabet or an independent science or technology. They have only built upon what Moors or Africans from North Africa, West Africa and as far south as Senegal gave them in Spain...

"This thing is about gatekeepers. They keep the truth from the masses of African people - which would change thoughts - which would change the actions (Africans appear to be) locked into now – which help to perpetuate white supremacy. African scholars who show us light have died as paupers instead of being acclaimed for their work."

Chancellor Williams, author of *Rebirth of African Civilization* and *The Destruction of Black Civilization*, Bro. Sekou explained, died broke and alone in Chicago. John G. Jackson, author of *Introduction to African Civilizations, Man, God and Civilization* and other great works, died a virtual pauper in a nursing home in

Chicago, he said. Joel A. Rogers, author of *World's Great Men of Color, Sex and Race, From Superman to Man* and other groundbreaking books, faired much better, according to Sekou. Although he and his work were ridiculed, he forged ahead, "saved his money, published his books himself and they sold."

Sister pioneers who managed to escape the blues, he said, include Dr. Charshee C.L. McIntyre, author of *Criminalizing a Race,* Prof. Francis Crest Welsing, author of *The Isis Papers* and Professor Marimba Ani, author of *Yurugu: An African-Centered Critique of European Cultural Thought and Behavior.*

"Dr. McIntyre went stealth until she got what she needed and then she hit. Prof. Welsing was fired from Howard University when she showed her hand but she continues to lecture and teach. Prof. Ani told me she went before a tenure review committee at Hunter College after her book was published. She said she did the appropriate rituals, wore white for purity, and felt that she and the ancestors would prevail. She got it and soon retired," he said. But, there are many tales of others who felt the sting of those who keep the gates, as Sekou explained.

According to Dr. Ben, his first mentor, scholar Arturo Schomburg, was driven to alcoholism under the pressure put on him over the years he attempted to uplift his people with a proper view of world history. He told a small group who came here recently to honor the memory of Dr. John Henrik Clarke, that Mr. Schomburg was systematically "pressured into selling" his extensive collection to New York Public Library for a fraction of its value. Dr. Ben said he and his good friend Dr. Clarke, author (coauthor) of *Africa, Lost and Found, African People at the Crossroads, Christopher Columbus and the African Holocaust* and *Who Betrayed the African Revolution,* were similarly pressured. He told the crowd about the strokes he and Clarke suffered in their drive to study, teach, and provide for their families. Dr. Clarke eventually lost his sight and Dr. Ben was unable to speak for 18 months following one of his strokes, he confessed to the audience.

The record shows, Trinidad-born C.L.R. James, author of *The Black Jacobins* and *A History of Pan-African Revolt,* was labeled an undesirable alien by the U.S. State Department in 1952 and interned on Ellis Island. He was later deported to Trinidad.

Walter Bridges, a New York based psychotherapist, said when we are talking about people who forge a way against those who impose, "We are talking plantation politics. You get you one, take his ass out there and string him up in front of everybody. Then you strip him down, beat him and show everybody the price that must be paid by those who want to stand against authority. The demonstration deters most. They begin to think about their mortgage and car payments today… The people who take the stand are heroes. Most heroes are dead. But those who stand do it because they want to," he said.

Prof. Ngemi described our scholarship movement in different regions of the world in near divine terms. He said African Scholars from Africa, the Americas and the Caribbean are establishing a new standard in documenting history. Bro Sekou agreed.

"The object of looking at history is not to point back to prove anything to white people," Sekou argued. "We look at history to show blacks that we came from people who were builders in control of the spiritual and socialization processes others are claiming. We look back to show what caused us to look like children in the face of Europeans…

"There is a story in ancient Egyptian literature that speaks to the sons and daughters of truth that are coming back to reclaim the thrown of truth – for truth. That is happening and there is nothing (falsehood) can do to stop it," he concluded.

APPENDIX J

Sidney Poitier Returns to *"The Door of No Return"*
By Lamont Muhammad, December 22, 2005

[Sidney Portier, "Tree of Return," Quidah, Benin, December 2005. Photo credit: Lamont Muhammad]

OUIDAH, Benin – Sidney Poitier, the distinguished actor and humanitarian recently traveled the same ancient, dusty road here, where half the Africans exported into chattel slavery walked in chains for centuries, historians here say.

Mr. Poitier and a contingent of other luminaries were in Benin to help draw attention to a successful Red Cross measles vaccination program, a recent study found, reduced cases of measles in 19 sub-Saharan African countries by 90 percent.

Pope Nicolas V issued the agreement that launched the African slave trade on January 8, 1454, according Martine de Souza, author of *Ouidah: A Bit of History*. Eventually, Portugal, France, England, Holland and Denmark built separate fortresses here to advance the horrific merchandizing of Africans with the help of African expansionist. The Europeans exchanged guns, canons, gunpowder and tobacco with African kings for captured Africans. The kings used the advanced weapons to conquer smaller kingdoms; and subsequently, winners sold losers to slave traders, in order to acquire more ammunition, which they used in turn to command more territory and more power.

Ouidah, described by Ms. de Souza as the largest African slave market hub on the infamous West African coast, is a major hub for Voodoo in the region. Many of the Africans exported from here during the slave era ended up in Brazil, Haiti and other corners in the

Caribbean and the Americas, taking along their practice of Voodoo. It continues to be a major practice here.

Benin is the former territory of the Dahomey. They were the expansionist whose victims were forced to walk in chains down this hot sandy-red trail that leads to the Atlantic sea coast. They came here in chains from as far away as Nigeria, on Benin's eastern border. They were held in markets from which the Europeans selected the so-called best breeds. "From the market the slaves were led down a path with several stops. The first was the *Tree of Forgetfulness*, the author of the pamphlet on Ouidah, de Sousa wrote. The ritual, rooted in Voodoo, required male slaves to go around the tree nine times. Women circumambulated the tree seven times to forget everything about their country, their origin, their culture, and their identity," de Sousa said. The slaves, it continued, were usually "placed in a dark room called *Zomai*, which means 'where the light is not allowed to go.' Sometimes people would wait in *Zomai* for many months, in complete darkness. Those who died there or who were too tired to travel were thrown in a mass grave," that is marked by a memorial here today. When it was time, survivors, according to the pamphlet, were forced further down the path to the next stop. "They would turn three times around the *Tree of Return*, in hopes of coming back in spirit. This marked the ultimate ritual, before their departure through the *"Door of No Return,"* the author said.

Seemingly touched, Mr. Poitier stopped at the *Tree of Return* and led a number of other Africans born in America around the tree three times to symbolize their physical return home, they said. Then the group continued down the path to the *Door of No Return*, where Mr. Poitier broke away from the group, walked his tall frame through the monument that straddles the end of the dusty red path today. Alone, he stared out across the Atlantic Ocean in silence for several minutes before returning to the group.

The Door of No Return was officially inaugurated here in 1994. In 1998 a group of elders and leading citizens here organized the first day of repentance and reconciliation. They "knelt down to ask God's forgiveness for the sins of those ancestors who cooperated with the slaves buyers," de Souza wrote. *The Door of Return*, the mayor here told this writer the day before, was designed to welcome Africans in the Diaspora back home.

The visit here capped off a grueling three-day measles vaccination initiative that was designed to inoculate one million children in Benin December 12 - 18. The initiative is a partnership headed by the American Red Cross (ARC), the United Nations Foundations, Centers for Disease Control and Prevention, the United Nations Children's Fund, and the World Health Organization. Other significant players include the International Federation of the Red Cross and Red Crescent Societies, the Canadian International Development

Agency and other countries and governments affected by measles.

Launched in 2001, the measles initiate is designed to "control measles deaths in Africa by vaccinating 200 million children and preventing 1.2 million deaths by 2006," planners said.

According to a September 2005 study published in the British medical journal, *The Lancet*, the initiative prevented 90,000 measles deaths in Africa in 2003. Prior to the initiative, according to the study, countries in the study reported an average of more than 164,000 measles cases. In 2003, after the implementation of the measles initiative, the participating countries reported a total of 15,619 cases. That is a 91 percent reduction of cases, according to the report.

Other heavy-hitters who traveled in the group with Mr. Poitier for the event included: Steven E. Carr, a member of the Board of Governors of the ARC; Kimberly Green, International Spokesperson for the Green Family Foundation Initiative, ARC; Robert A. Fippinger, Orrick, Herrington and Sutcliffe, law firm partner; Donna Garland, Director of the Office of Enterprise Communication; Dr. Mark Grabowsky, the Senior Advisor to International Services Department of the ARC/Measles Initiative; and Sherry Lansing, founder and chair of the Sherry Lansing Foundation, and former chair of Paramount Pictures (1992 – 2005).

Mr. Poitier, who said he will turn 79-years of age on February 20, 2006, said he was invited to participate in the program by his good friend, Ms. Lansing. But, he said, he has been a supporter of the ARC for 62 years.

"When I was in need of assistance (62 years ago), the Red Cross was the organization that came to my aid... I have since that time been a friend and supporter of the Red Cross," the humble giant said.

APPENDIX K

Do Vaccines Cure or Kill?
by Lamont Muhammad
03.22.06

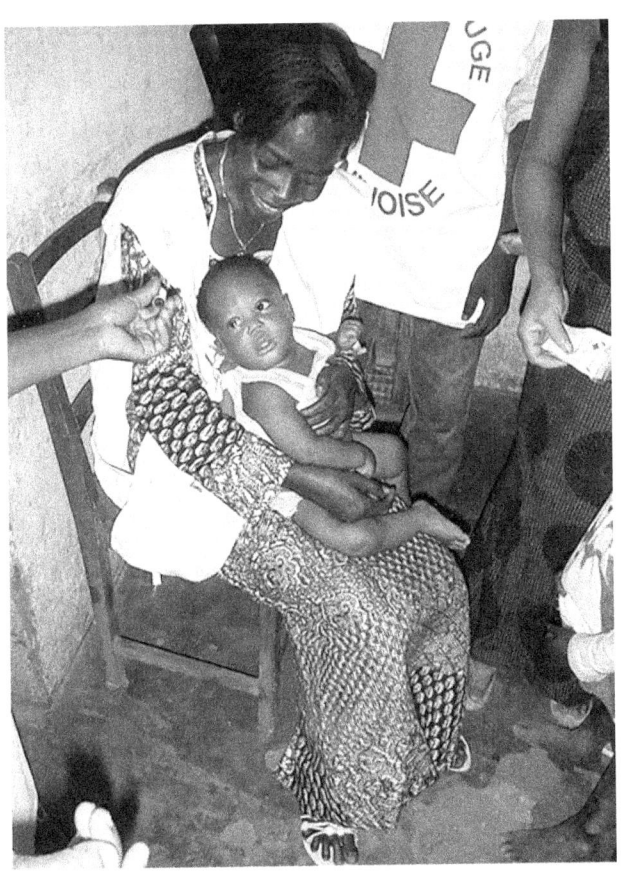

[Child anticipates receiving a measles vaccine in the village of Allada in Benin, December 2005. Photo credit: Lamont Muhammad]

BENIN, West Africa - The American Red Cross (ARC) invited legendary actor Sidney Poitier and other luminaries here in December 2005, to draw attention to an initiative the ARC launched in 2001 to control measles deaths in Africa. The ultimate goal, planners said, is to vaccinate a total of 200 million (Sub-Sahara African) children by 2006. The immediate goal, they said, is to vaccinate 100 million children age 15 years and under December 12 to 18.

Critics of vaccines and the pharmaceutical industry want to know who is really benefiting from these initiatives and what diseases are going to show up in the recipients of the vaccines years later. Dr. Jack Felder, a biochemist and a retired New York City school teacher had one question when he heard about the project in Benin.

"You mean the ARC, which hardly did a thing for Black people in New Orleans after Hurricane Katrina, now wants to go 9,000 miles to save Black people in Africa from measles?

Mr. Poitier, 79, described himself as "a longtime supporter of the ARC." He said he had been invited to participate in the "Benin Measles Campaign" by his good friend Sherry Lansing, founder and chair of the Sherry Lansing Foundation, and former chair of Paramount Pictures (1992 – 2005). ARC board members and organizers, some private sector representatives and three journalists visited a number of vaccination sites and governmental ministries in Cotonou and Porto Novo, the capital here, from December 12 to 14. According to volunteer organizers on the ground in the villages, the turn out for the vaccinations was good. The incentives, in certain villages, included elaborate pomp and ceremony, including voodoo.

"Initially, people were wary of the program," said one of the volunteers in the village of Allada. She spoke French, the official language here, which was translated for the English-speaking participants by ARC personnel. "Since 2001 people have seen that those children who took the vaccines are still alive," she explained, smiling broadly, "and they see incidence of measles have lowered. They have become believers… We are having a great turn out," she said.

When Dr. Gregory Muhammad, of the Abundant Life Clinic in Phoenix, Arizona, was asked, via telephone recently, to offer an opinion on vaccines he deferred to the title of a book, *Murder by Injection*, by Eustace Mullins. The author argues in the book that vaccinations are one of the "holy waters" of a global medical church. It describes the church as a global predator that is more interested in making money than healing people, Dr. Muhammad said of the book. Dr. Cass Ingram, author of *The Cause for Cancer Revealed…the vaccination connection*, agrees with that argument. He wrote in his book that vaccines cause more diseases than they cure.

"Entire diseases are largely due to the toxic consequences of vaccinations: autism, attention deficit, fibromyalgia, chronic fatigue syndrome, polymyositis (inflamation of the heart sac), Alzheimer's disease, Parkinson's disease, lymphoma, juvenile diabetes, multiple sclerosis, and various cancers. Is this anything other than professional tyranny of the greatest degree? ...Vaccines are directly tied to cancer, in fact, they outright cause it. Thus, how could such medicines be beneficial?" (From pages 15 and 16, The Cause for Cancer Revealed,,,)

According to Dr. Ingram vaccines are made from parasitic viruses that are derived from animals. The problem begins with the fact that modern science has no idea of what a virus actually is.

"This is the kind of bizarre machine of synthesis that a virus is-there is nothing else like it in nature. It fully adapts itself to its host, becoming a part of it. Yet, while doing so it damages it. What's more, if circumstances are right, it will kill it," Ingram wrote (pg.14).

Dr. Mark Grabowsky, the Senior Advisor to the International Services Department of the ARC/Measles Initiative in Africa admitted to this writer that he does not take vaccines when he travels. If or when he gets sick while traveling in places like Africa, he said, he submits to the appropriate medical procedure to heal but avoids vaccines.

Nevertheless, Dr. Grabowsky and other members of the ARC team were hailed as dedicated soldiers in the battle to lower the death rate for children in Africa at the final dinner here.

According to a September 2005 British medical study published in *The Lancet*, the initiative prevented 90,000 measles deaths in Africa in 2003. Prior to the initiative, according to the study, countries in the study reported an average of more than 164,000 measles cases. In 2003, after the implementation of the measles initiative, the participating countries reported a total of 15,619 cases - a 91 percent reduction of cases, according to the report.

The ARC described the initiative as a partnership it heads that includes the United Nations Foundations, Centers for Disease Control and Prevention, the United Nations Children's Fund, and the World Health Organization. Other significant players include the International Federation of the Red Cross and Red Crescent Societies, the Canadian International Development Agency and other countries and governments affected by measles.

Mr. Poitier said he has been a supporter of the ARC for decades. "When I was in need of assistance (62 years ago), the Red Cross was the organization that came to my aid," he recalled outside one of the vaccination posts in Tori-Bossito. "I have since that time been a friend and supporter of the Red Cross," he told reporters, adding that the developed world has the capacity to aid the developing world and should.

The humble giant's itinerary also included a visit to *The Door of No Return* in Ouidah, from where many were shipped into the Atlantic slave trade, and a visit with a friend here.

APPENDIX L

Apocalypto: *And the Missing Link*
By Lamont Muhammad
2.6.07

Mel Gibson's *Apocalypto*, plays like a thinly veiled composite of the hidden centuries of the Aboriginal Black "Indian" history of ancient Mexico, in two hours and 19 minutes of blood and gore.

To its credit, the movie does show there was a hand full of Black people in Mexico before the Europeans stumbled into the Americas looking for India.

Some may ask: How did Blacks get to Mexico before the Trans-Atlantic slave trade?

Unfortunately, the controversial Mr. Gibson, fails to explain that the few Blacks who were sprinkled in the backdrop of the Maya slave market scenes in the movie were depicting the descendants of the first family of folks who actually built most of the pyramids there in ancient times.

"A number of scholars believe that for several centuries the invading Mongoloids uprooted and exterminated many of the resident Africoids. In addition to this, it is highly likely that many of the Blacks who escaped extermination or expulsion from their lands (in the Americas) probably 'mixed and melted into the billion-bodied Mongoloid gene pool,'" wrote Legrand H. Clegg II, in his essay: *The First Americans*. It was published in Ivan Van Sertima's *African Presence in Early America*.

Apocalypto fades in with a quote from W. Durant: *A great civilization is not conquered from without until it has destroyed itself from within.* The action in the movie centers on the human struggle to overcome and control fear, or fall prey to slavery, suffering and death.

It tells the story of an indigenous community in Mexico that is suddenly invaded by savage-types. The invaders burn the village down, kill, maim, and torture their victims. The adults who survive the brutal invasion are tied-up, bound in tow, and marched off to a distant slave market center where some will be sacrificed to the gods. The children were left to fend for themselves in the forest without shelter.

The protagonist, Jaguar Paw, is among the captives. He miraculously defies the savage's attempts to kill him and kills a beloved of them in order to make his escape. Now they are driven by a vengeful determination to catch and kill Jaguar Paw. The nail biting chase ends when Jaguar Paw and his two remaining pursuers emerge from the jungle onto the shores of the Caribbean Sea. Exhausted, they are struck by a number of large sailing vessels anchored off shore, and the strange White people approaching the beach in rowboats. The savages were fixated on the ships and walked toward the new people. But Jaguar Paw was still on his mission. He escaped the beach, rescued his family from a pit, and took them further into the forest to start "a new beginning."

Gibson, the celebrated actor and producer of the most successful independent movie of all time, *The Passion of Christ*, was said to have been inspired to make *Apocalypto*, after watching a documentary on the Maya, Archaeologist Richard Hansen told the January/February 2007 edition of *ARCHEOLOGY* Magazine. *Dawn of the Maya*, showed much of what has been unearthed at an ancient Maya site in Mexico's Yucatan by a team of archeologists headed by Mr. Hansen. The research "showed the incredible economic and political power the people at the site were wielding, and then we see their total demise, a complete abandonment of these systems." Henson told *ARCHEOLOGY*. He said Gibson telephoned him after seeing the documentary because he "saw a message there for humanity." Most of the actors in the film are Yucatec Maya and the entire dialog is spoken in that tongue.

Thanks to researchers like Mr. Clegg and Runoko Rashidi, modern researchers can see the savages who attacked Jaguar Paw and his people were Clegg's "Mongoloids" who came to the Americas through the Bering Strait and murdered and raped the Black Indians into the Hollywood version of the American Indian. History shows they had already slaughtered Black folks into near extinction in China over the centuries, evidenced by the fact that the oldest fossils found there are of Black folks, and, according to the 1968 edition of the University of Chicago's Encyclopedia Britannica, the first three dynasties in ancient China were made up of Black people.

Dr. Cheikh Anta Diop, the late renowned historian and scientist described Mongoloids as a product of mixing between Black and White, according to a piece by James Brunson, titled: *African Presence in Early China*, published in Prof. Van Sertima's *African Presence in Early Asia*. That is another long story, but a careful reading of history shows Blacks traveled the earth first, and then Yellow folks discovered the earth is round, and then White people became enlightened. That is the missing link to Gibson's brilliant piece, which I truly enjoyed.

Apocalypto is Greek for "an unveiling and a new beginning." That sounds good. But in Biblical terms, Apocalypse represents "an imminent cosmic cataclysm in which God destroys the ruling powers of evil and raises the righteous to life in a messianic kingdom," according to Webster's Collegiate (10th edition) Dictionary.

I am looking forward to that "blockbuster."

APPENDIX M

(The Alamo, 2007. Photo credit: Lamont Muhammad)

Juneteenth
by Lamont Muhammad
06.22.07

SAN ANTONIO, Texas – Juneteenth was celebrated here this year near the Alamo, a symbol of this nation's expansionism into the Americas, and a determination on the part of some here to expand the institution of slavery in the early 1800s.

On June 19, 1865, two-years and five months after President Abraham Lincoln issued the Emancipation Proclamation, the citizens of Texas were finally informed that slavery had been ended. The date has since been celebrated as Juneteenth, the day black slaves were freed, and white folks were forced to let them go in Texas.

Byron Miller, the founder and Commissioner of the San Antonio Juneteenth Association, told an audience along the famed River Walk here that it took two years and five months to announce the abolishment of slavery in Texas because it took that long to insure there were enough troops here to enforce the order.

Texas declared itself independent of Mexico in 1836, because the Mexican government was determined to enforce the fact that slavery had been abolished there in 1821. Led by Americans who wanted to rob Mexico and expand slavery, Texas declared itself the "Lone Star Republic" (1836). The Mexican government responded by sending General Santa Anna and 2,500 troops crush the rebellion at the Alamo. Some 200, mostly United States (US) citizens, including Bill Travis, Jim Bowie, and Davie Crockett, were slaughtered and defeated on March 5, 1836. The only survivors, according to *The Alamo*, by Stephen Ortman, were a few women, children and a slave named Joe. They were given blankets and money and told to warn all rebels that they were about to meet the same fate as those who died at the Alamo, Mr. Ortman wrote.

Of course, Gen. Sam Houston tracked Santa Ana down and defeated the Mexican Army three weeks later near

Houston, Texas. The US annexed Texas in 1846, which triggered the Mexican – American War. After the war the US took half of Mexico, including "California, Nevada, Utah, Arizona, New Mexico, most of Colorado, and parts of Kansas, Oklahoma, and Wyoming." (Ortman) The wealthy Governor of the Mexican state of California, at the time, was Pio Pico. He was of African descent. His family had settled and owned most of modern day Los Angeles. He died a pauper there under US rule.

Fortunately, there were opponents to the US robbing of half of Mexico, especially for the purpose of expanding slavery and increasing the number of slave states in Washington. General Ulysses S. Grant described the US crime against Mexico in his autobiography in these terms.

"For myself, I was bitterly opposed to the measure (taking of Texas), and to this day regard the war, which resulted, as one of the most unjust ever waged by a stronger against a weaker nation...

"To us it was an empire and of incalculable value; but it might have been obtained by other means. The Southern rebellion was largely the outgrowth of the Mexican war. Nations, like individuals, are punished for their transgressions. We got our punishment in the most sanguinary and expensive war of modern times." (Ortman)

Texas was the last state to surrender to the Union at the end of the Civil War. Texans fought hard to maintain slavery, especially here where cotton was king. In fact, Alamo is a Spanish word for Cotton Tree.

Nevertheless, on June 19, 1865, "Union Major General Gordon Granger stood on the balcony of the Ashton Villa Hotel in Galveston, Texas and read General Order #3.

"'The people of Texas are informed that in accordance with a Proclamation by the Executive of the United States, all slaves are free.'

"With those words, more than 200,000 Texas men, women and children of African descent were freed, signaling the end of slavery," the *2007 Juneteenth Celebration Guide*, by the *African-American Reflections Newspaper* here, said.

One hundred and forty-two years later, the children of the slave masters and the children of the slaves celebrate together. Mr. Miller told the crowd that Juneteenth freed Black people from slavery, "and freed white folks from the immoral practice..."

APPENDIX N

A Snapshot of the Theology of the Nation of Islam

[*Master W. Fard Muhammad*]

My name is W. F. Muhammad
I came to North America by myself.
My uncle was brought over here by
the Trader three hundred seventy-nine
years ago.

*My uncle cannot talk his own Language
He does not know that he is my uncle.
He likes the Devil because the Devil gives him nothing.
Why does he like the Devil?
Because the Devil put fear in him when he was a little boy.
Why does he fear, now, since he is a big man?
Because the Devil taught him to eat the wrong food.*

[English Lesson No. C1: 1-10] [131]

A Brief History:

Master Wallace D. Fard Muhammad founded the Nation of Islam (NOI) in "Black Bottom" Detroit, Michigan, during the "Great Depression," on July 4, 1930. He was born on February 26, 1877, just outside of the Holy City Mecca, Saudi Arabia, the son of a wealthy black cloth merchant, and a white mother from the area of today's Caucasus Mountains.

Master Fard said he studied 42 years in preparation to deliver black people. He spoke some sixteen languages and a variety of dialects. He first entered the U.S. in 1910, acquired a degree from U.C.L.A., traveled to different corners of the world and returned to the U.S. to proclaim the birth of the Nation of Islam. He began, first, by going door to door, telling the poor people who

---

[131] Elijah Muhammad, *Supreme Wisdom*, English Lesson No. C1: 1-10

let him in that he was selling "silk from your people in the East." Then he began to teach them about their great past, how to eat properly and how to love and respect each other. "He understood that the Bible was the religious book best known to his followers and cleverly utilized it to verify his description of the black people's history and the white people's doom," wrote Richard Brent Turner, in his book, *Islam In the African-American Experience*.[132]

Mother Clara Muhammad, the wife of Elijah Muhammad, was the first person in their family to meet the cloth merchant, according to their author grandson.

> *One of grandmother's lady friends brought a man around to the house who sold fabrics and a red cloth that some of them were putting in their windows. Grandmother told of how she was sitting on her back porch one afternoon when she saw "The Savior" (a reference that she would use emphatically, Master W.D. Fard Muhammad. "He looked to me like a poor white man."*

His first question was, "Where is brother (Grandfather)?"

Her reply: "He's in the house asleep lying across the bed drunk as a coot.

---

[132] Richard Brent Turner, *Islam In the African-American Experience*, Indiana University Press, 1997, p. 149

Master Fard told his students the history he was teaching came from the ancient archives of the Ottoman Empire. He said he was privileged to read some before the records were destroyed, according to a grandson of the Honorable Elijah Muhammad, Jesus Muhammad-Ali, author of *The Evolution of the Nation of Islam*. He said the Islamic Empire destroyed many secrets recorded in the archives from fear the info would fall into the hands of their enemies. The Ottoman Empire fell in 1923.

Mr. Muhammad, born Robert Poole on October 7, 1897, in Bold springs, Georgia, was the son of a Baptist Preacher. He escaped the south and moved to Detroit with his father, great grandfather and older brother to seek employment in the auto industry in 1923.[133] In 1929, when the Great Depression began he was among the great ranks of the unemployed. Mother Clara convinced her husband to attend Fard's next meeting, at which Elijah immediately recognized Fard in divine terms. He joined the N.O.I., began to clean himself up and eventually became Fard's most trusted confidant. Fard taught Elijah day and night, for 3 and a half years, according to NOI records. Soon, Fard would be run away by U.S. federal authorities.

> *The letter from the U.S. Immigration came in the spring of 1934. Master Fard was told if he did not leave within 14 days he would face deportation, "due to unrest stemming from his activities in the Negro community."*

---
[133] Ibid p. 26

Grandfather and the family had moved twice. They were in a much nicer home, in a more respectable area of Detroit. Master Fard summoned the Minister's staff and told them to obey Grandfather as Supreme Minister and uncle Kallatt as Supreme Captain. They did not need

[The Most Honorable Elijah Muhammad, courtesy of the U.S. Library of Congress online/ Final Call news.]

him anymore. The afternoon on May 24, 1934, would be the last time they would

> see Master Fard with the exception of Grandfather. A week or so later Grandfather received a telegram: Master Fard wanted him to come and see him in a Chicago jail. He told Grandfather that the family should move to Chicago... Master Fard then told Grandfather why he sent for him. "I wanted you to see me here behind these bars. If you follow me, this is where you will find yourself."[134]

Mr. Muhammad became the new leader of the N.O.I. He spent the first seven years of his ministry fending off rivals for the top spot and ducking death plots by many, including those from his own brother Khallat [135] and the U.S. federal authorities. In 1942, during WWII, Elijah and his oldest son Emmanuel were convicted of sedition and Selective Service violations for teaching against the war. They were incarcerated in the federal penitentiary in Milan, Michigan, form 1942 to 1946 where they converted many prisoners to Islam.[136] By the 1950's Mr. Muhammad, with the help of dynamic ministers, including Minister Malcolm X, he was successfully building "a nation within a nation."

> (T)he LESSONS that OUR SAVIOUR (ALLAH) gave us to Study and Learn is the Fulfillment of the Prophesies of All the Former Prophets concerning the

---
[134] Ibid, p. 35-36
[135] Ibid, p. 167
[136] Ibid, p, 168

> *Beginning of the Devils, the Ending of
> the Civilization, and of our Enslavement
> by the Devils, and Present Time of our
> Delivery from the Devils by OUR
> SAVIOUR (ALLAH). Praise his holy name!
> There is no God but Allah. How that
> ALLAH would Separate us from the Devils
> and then, Destroy them; and Change us
> into a new and Perfect People; and
> Fill the Earth with FREEDOM, JUSTICE,
> AND EQUALITY as it was filled
> with wickedness; and Making we, the Poor
> Lost-Founds, the Perfect RULERS...*[137]

Mr. Muhammad put his followers into a rigid self-improvement program and lined them in ranks. Carnal weapons were forbidden. By the 1960s, again, through the dynamic advocacy of Min. Malcolm and later Min. Louis X (Farrakhan), Mr. Muhammad had begun to attract a broader range of supporters, including black professionals to the cause. he subsequently assembled an international trade network for the benefit of Black people. By the early 1970s, he had a network of schools and businesses that generated $27 to $30 million a year for the NOI and the Black people who supported it.

> *Just think about it, it was the most
> beautiful thing. The emissaries go down
> and make the initial purchase for the
> Nation of Islam coffers that had been*

---

[137] Elijah Muhammad, *Instructions given to Laborer, excerpt of #3*

developed by people giving in charity. The fish is purchased in Peru. At any one time, there were twenty to thirty ships on the high seas going back and forth. The fish came into twelve to eighteen ports around the United States. it was handled by the temple, and all temples would purchase the fish from the central temple in Chicago; But now that fish has to be sold, So the profit is going to be made by the local temple. This provided jobs for brothers who couldn't get work. they converted various trucks into cold-storage fish trucks.

This was happening all over the country. It was one of the most fantastic things I'd ever seen in my life, and this little black man with a third-grade education was showing the world. It was an economic system.

Elijah Muhammad raised Lazarus up. Lazy, stiff-necked, rebellious-he got up off his behind and did something.[138]

****

[138] Steve Barboza, *American Jihad, Go Buy Fish,* Doubleday, p. 100

The following chronology is a thumbnail sketch of the *Supreme Wisdom* of the Nation of Islam (NOI), as taught by the Honorable Elijah Muhammad, officially, since 1934.

The first question in the "Student Enrollment (Rules of Islam)," is: "Who is the Original man?" The answer is given: "The Original man is the Asiatic black man; the Maker; the Owner; The Cream of the planet Earth – God of the Universe."

The second question is: "Who is the Colored man?" The answer is given: "The Colored man is the Caucasian (white man). Or, Ya(ku)b's grafted Devil – the Skunk of the planet Earth."

Mr. Muhammad, known by his followers as the "Messenger of God," was a fearless little person who defined Almighty God, Allah, as a sleeping Black man who allowed his dissatisfied children (White and Yellow people) to rule the earth for a time that has been exhausted. His common sense and eye opening rhetoric attracted brilliant helpers to the cause like Ministers: James Shabazz, "the Sun of Thunder;" Jeremiah Shabazz; Malcolm X; Clarence 13X (founder of the Five Percent Nation); Louis Farrakhan; and untold other great human beings that went after their vision of helping the Messenger of Allah.

The Original man, according to Muhammad, has no birth record. There was no one around to record the event of God creating Himself out of the triple darkness of space. The first recorded event occurred 78 trillion years ago with the making of a star/or Sun.

The next major event occurred some 66 trillion years ago, when a Black scientist, Tipu, set off an explosion that separated our Moon from Asia (Earth). Tipu was angry with the people because they would not submit to speak one language. Therefore, he attempted to destroy the planet. Nevertheless, a segment of the people survived and our Moon began to circle Asia.

The blasting away of MOON by an enemy that robbed the MOON of its (water) and poured it onto this part of the planet Earth can also be compared to the evil white slave-traders, guided by John Hawkins, the explorer, to come among us and take us by force and bring us to this part of our Earth among strangers whom our fathers knew not. In so doing they made us lose all knowledge of our self and our kind, like this man or God who in his frenzy to try to force to try to force all of the people to believe as he believed and to speak the same language with no difference in dialect, caused the deportation of the MOON from the Earth. So it is with our enemy today. He wants us all to kneel and bow to his way of life and if he cannot get us to do so he wants to be rid of us and our Earth.[139]

The next major event happened 50,000-years ago when another scientist, Shabazz, led a large group of people out of the fertile and civilized Nile Valley and into jungles to make them tough. The Messenger said he saw down the line of time and realized his people had to be made to survive the future. Members of the "Tribe of Shabazz" are known to have nappy hair, broad noses and thick lips – features they acquired in jungles where their diets changed. They are also known to be physically strong.

Sixteen thousand years ago, Mr. Muhammad said, a segment of our original family was banished from India, and forced to cross the Bering Strait from East Asia to West Asia (America).

Ten-thousand-years later, or 6,000 years ago, according to Muhammad, a man was born who was determined to make a new man to replace the rulers of the day.

> *Here we have a black man, who is the original man, of whom, we can't locate his birth; he's the aboriginal human being of the Earth. Now from him he has produced brown, yellow, red and white, through the master wisdom of grafting of the God, Yakub.*[140]

---

[139] Muhammad, Elijah, *The Flag of Islam*. The Final Call Inc. 1983, p. 14
[140] Muhammad, Elijah. *Yakub: The Father of Mankind*. Secretarius. 2002, p. 70

Mr. Yakub, the "Big Head Scientist," as he was called, was a Black man who attracted his followers from "dissatisfied" members of the society, like himself. He promised those who followed him he would lead them to a life of luxury, by making slaves of others. His followers were also required to adhere to a birth control program that transformed them from black to brown to yellow and finally to pale skin, blue eyed blonds, Mr. Muhammad's *Supreme Wisdom* said. By age 16, Yakub had graduated all of the colleges in Mecca, and he took his doctrine to the streets.

The authorities, however, feared such teachings and subsequently arrested and persecuted him and his followers. When the prisons filled with Yakub's people the King visited him in prison and asked what could be worked out to end the trouble. Yakub asked the King to give him and his followers, money and other necessities of life for 20 years. The King agreed and ordered that all Yakub's followers be rounded up and loaded on ships. They sailed to the island of Pelan or Patmos in the Aegean Sea.

> *Yakub's First Rule was to see that all his followers were healthy, strong and good breeders. If not, he sent them back (all that he found that was not good in multiplying), and that they should marry at the age of sixteen.*

Next, Yakub gave his people the Law on Birth Control-to be enforced while manufacturing the Devil. That was to destroy the alike and save the unlike, which means kill the (black babies) and save the brown babies. The Law was given to the doctors, the ministers, the nurses and cremator.

The Doctor's Law was to examine all that marry. And this was his law: That anyone desiring to marry must, first, be qualified by the doctor and, in turn, he qualified or disqualified them to the minister.

The Minister would marry only the ones that were unlike.

The Nurse's Law was to kill the black babies at birth by sticking a needle in the brain of the babies or feed it to some wild beast; and tell the mother that her baby was an angel baby and that it was only taken to heaven; and someday when the mother dies, her baby would have secured her a home in heaven. But save all the brown ones and tell their mother that she was lucky that her baby was a holy baby; and she should take good care

> *of her baby, educate it, and that some day it would be a great man.*
>
> *All nurses, doctors and ministers- Yakub put them under a death penalty who failed to carry out the Law as it was given them.*
>
> *Also, the Cremator, who would burn the black babies when the nurse brought (them) to him.*
>
> *Also, death for them if they revealed the Secret.*
>
> *He also had other rules and laws which are not mentioned in this Lesson.* [141]

Yakub lived for 150 years, but his plan took 600-years to manifest the change. When his followers completed his instructions, a group of them (white skin, blond hair and blue eyes) set sail for the garden of paradise their Black ancestors had been expelled from 600-years earlier.

The original people saw the "unlike" (White) people as angels.

> *Mr. Yakub taught his made devils on Pelan: "That –when you go back to the holy black nation, rent a room in*

---

[141] Muhammad, Elijah. *Lost-Found Muslim Lesson No. 2,* Answer No. 28

their homes. Teach your wives to go out the next morning around the neighbors of people, and tell that you heard her talking about them last night.

"When you have got them fighting and killing each other, then ask them to let you help settle their disputes, and restore peace among them. If they agree, then you will be able to rule them both." This method the white race practices on the black nation, the world over. They upset their peace by putting one against the other, and then rule them after dividing them.

This is why the so-called American so-called Negroes can never agree on unity among themselves, which would put them on top overnight. The devils keep them divided by paid informers from among themselves. They keep such fools among us. But, the real truth of the devils sometimes converts the informers and brings them over to us as true believers. We don't bother about killing them, as I am not teaching that which I want to be kept

> *as a secret, but that which the world has not known and should know.*
>
> *After Yakub's devils were among the Holy people of Islam (the black nation) for six months, they had our people at war with each other. The holy people were unable to understand, just why they could not get along in peace with each other, until they took the matter to the King.*
>
> *The King told the holy people of the black nation that the trouble they were having was caused by the white devils in their midst, and that there would be no peace among them until they drove these white made devils from among them.*[142]

That recognition on the part of the King led to the second banishment of Yakubs' people 600-years and six months after the first. This time they did not leave in boats. This time they were stripped and made to walk into a hostile seclusion in the caves and hillsides of Europe.

> *We ran the Devils over the Arabian Desert. We took from them everything except the language and made him walk*

---
[142] Muhammad, Elijah. *Message to the Blackman*. 1965, p. 116=117

every step of the way. It was twenty-two hundred miles. He went savage and lived in the caves of Europe. Eu means hillsides and Rope is the rope to bind in. It was six thousand years ago.

Mossa (Moses) came two thousand years later and taught him how to live a respectful life, how to build a home for himself and some of the Tricknology that Yakub taught him, which was devilishment-telling lies, stealing and how to master the original man.

Mossa was a half-original, a prophet, which was predicted by the Twenty-Three Scientists in the year, One - fifteen thousand nineteen years ago today.[143]

*The Most Honorable Elijah Muhammad (c) in the Sudan 1959
(Photo courtesy of Akbar Muhammad)*

---

[143] Muhammad, Elijah. *Lost-Found Muslim Lesson No. 1*, Excerpted from answer/no. 4.

Illustrations:

Front page - design by Louigi Turton,
A.G.E.S. Logo design by Kamal Robinson
Title page – "Pops," by L. Muhammad
1-Monolithic Head San Lorenzo, Vera Cruz,
　Mexico, Courtesy Maya Website/ www...　5
2- Hortencia Zapata Bacho at her Ocaso
　Restaurant, by L. Muhammad　9
3- Asucena, by L. Muhammad　15
4- Marcelino and family, by L. Muhammad　16
5- Adam in Belize, by L. Muhammad　17
6- Map of Southern Mexico　18
7- Devil Dance, by L. Muhammad　21
8- Julio Aqustino, by L. Muhammad　22
9- Faces of Cuajinicuilapa　25
10- Police, by Lamont Muhammad　26
11- Mexican Stamps　47
13 - Sufferers Collogue : a/Children of Flower's
　Bank, Belize, 1999; b/Children playing
　in Cuajiniquilapa, Mexico, 1998; c/Children
　on bike in Lake Independence, Belize City,
　1999; d/Happy children in Lake
　Independence, Belize, 1999; e/Children
　running from tourists on Cape Coast, Ghana,
　1996; f/Children playing in Caribbean Sea
　inside the reef in Belize, Ambergris Caye,
　1995. All photos by Lamont Muhammad　49,50
14- Olmec Head , Courtesy Maya Website　51
15- Xunantunich, Belize, by Barry Tessman　53
16- Ego Hayes at home, 2002, by L. Muhammad　66

17- Reenactment of Garifuna Settlement Day 74
18- Garifuna in Belize, by L. Muhammad 75
19- Garifuna makes fu-fu 76
20- Brother Candy, by L. Muhammad 78, 79
21- Pyramid Collogue: Xunatunich, Belize, by Barry Tessman; Author in Giza, Egypt, 1994, By James Muhammad, Miamisburg "Monks" Mound, Ohio; Sakkara Pyramid, Egypt; and Author's son at Lamanai, Belize, 1995, by L. Muhammad 96, 97
22- Ras Nelson, 2002, by L. Muhammad 99
22a- Dr. Charles S. Finch III by L. Muhammad 105
23- Author's son 137
24- Her Highness Verdiacee Tiari Washitaw-Turner Goston El-Bey, by L. Muhammad 163
25- Seth Muhammad, Louisiana, 2000, by L. Muhammad 168
26- – Patricia Pena and Maria Callejas Salinas in Harlem, 2001, by L. Muhammad 177
27- MaVynee Betsch, 2001, by Linda Fletcher 185
28– Women at work in Nima, Ghana, 1996, by Lamont Muhammad 191
29- Collogue: 54th Massachusetts volunteer Infantry Re-enactors Company; Ranger Ralph Smith sports the regalia of Black Seminoles; Dr. Jack Felder on 125th Street in Harlem, 2001; Head slave quarters on Kingsley Plantation, Florida; Ruins of tabby cement slave cabins on Kingsley Plantation, 2001; A view from

the beach of black area on American Beach, Amelia Island, Florida; American Beach Black History Museum, 2001; The Black History Museum; Factories stain the sky near Jacksonville, Florida; Linda Fletcher (right), interviews Kitty Wilson Evans of the Historical Center of York County, South Carolina, at Kingsley Plantation, 2001; photos by L. Muhammad   205 - 207

30- Professor Ivan Van Sertima in Belize, 2000, by L. Muhammad   215

31- Sydney Poitier, 2005, by L. Muhammad   221

32- Child in Benin, 2005, by L. Muhammad   227

33- The Alamo, 2007, by Lamont Muhammad   237

34- Master W. F. Muhammad; NOI archives online   241

35-The Hon. Elijah Muhammad; courtesy of the Final Call news   245

36-The Hon. Elijah Muhammad in the Sudan; courtesy of Akbar Muhammad   257

Acknowledgments

I thank the Lord of the All of the Worlds for the Most Honorable Elijah Muhammad and his Ministers for declaring that Black people, including the Indians, are the original people of the earth and that Black people are at the root of all civilizations. "Everywhere others have traveled in the earth," Mr. Muhammad said, (they have discovered that) Black people had already been there."

I thank Stretch Lightburn, the Final Call Newspaper, Minister Muhammad Abdullah Muhammad, Bro. Adam, Gina Scott, Louigi Turton, Bryan Sullivan, Minister Gabree Amlac, and Michelle Neal for the first edition.

I am thankful to Sister Valerie E. Muhammad, Dr. Gregory Muhammad, Seth Muhammad, Minister Jabril Muhammad (the believers of Mosque #32), Her Highness Verdiacee Tiari Washitaw – Turner Goston El-Bey (PBUH), members of the Washitaw Nation, many members of the Nation of Islam, and Walter "Doc Bongo" Bridgers, M.S.W.

Of course, I must thank the Lord of the Worlds for the people of Belize, beginning with the mother of my children, Paula Joy Wagner Curry - who blessed me with Kamal Robinson, Jihaad, Jamilah, Tarik and Azizah Curry. Paula introduced me to the "Land of the Gods," as the ancient Maya called Belize. That sub-tropical paradise borders Mexico on the southeastern tip of the Yucatan Peninsula.

Special thanks must go to Joy Elliott, Bro. Victor Mansur Muhammad Mims, the unofficial Mayor of Clay Avenue in the Bronx – the late Mr. Henry Danner, the late Sis. Pah'Ti, Bro. Edwin "Bic" Hendricks, Sis. Linda Adjua Fletcher, Bro./Min. J.D. Muhammad, and Bro./Min. Ray Muhammad. Their assistance in this project is not measurable.

Also, I must thank Brother and author Hakim Hasan who contributed suggestions to the final structuring of this book and to author Mfundishi for his Foreword.

I am so very thankful to Allah for a Sister I have known from childhood. Patricia Burton's editing input and her "eagle eyes" helped to make this effort more reader friendly.

Finally, much appreciation goes to Bro. Raymond Sharrieff Muhammad, Editor in Chief of W.O.M.B. Publications for his editorial (Introduction), and for his proficiency in finalizing the final draft and putting a period to this project.

I Thank Allah for you All!!

ABOUT THE AUTHOR

Lamont Muhammad grew up in the South Bronx, New York City. His extended family included the Harlem based Minisink program, in which he was a member of Tapawingo and the Order of the Feather (1965), which introduced him to – and nurtured him on – Native American and African culture.

In 1968 he pledged to and became a member of the Black Enlightenment Fraternity, at Queens College. He later directed cultural, and educational youth programs for Settlement organizations in Boston and New York City.

Bro. Lamont was introduced to the teachings of the Honorable Elijah Muhammad, under the leadership of the Hon. Louis Farrakhan in 1979, and subsequently completed a journalism internship at the Trans-Urban News Service in Brooklyn, New York.

Since that time he has contributed to and worked for newspapers and magazines to record issues and events relevant to Black people especially, and human beings in general. His contributions include: *Africa Diaspora*, *Tradewinds*, *Focus*, *Indianapolis Visions* and *Dawn* Magazine(s). Newspapers include: *People's Voice*, *Big Red*, the *Indianapolis Recorder*, the *Baltimore Afro-American*, the *New York Amsterdam News*, *Amandala Press* (Belize), *The Black World Today* (www.tbwt.org) and the *Final Call*

(*FCN*), which he has contributed to since 1982. Bro. Lamont was the United Nations (UN) correspondent for *FCN* from 1993 to 1996, focusing on Africa, the Caribbean and developing nations.

The freelance journalist, author, teacher, long time organizer, student, founder and president of Ancient Geographic Expression Systems, continues to seek and document the common African foundation of this world and the ultimate destiny of modern cultures, by God's Grace.

www.ingramcontent.com/pod-product-compliance
Lightning Source LLC
Chambersburg PA
CBHW051040160426
43193CB00010B/1017